MARKET DAY

James Sturm

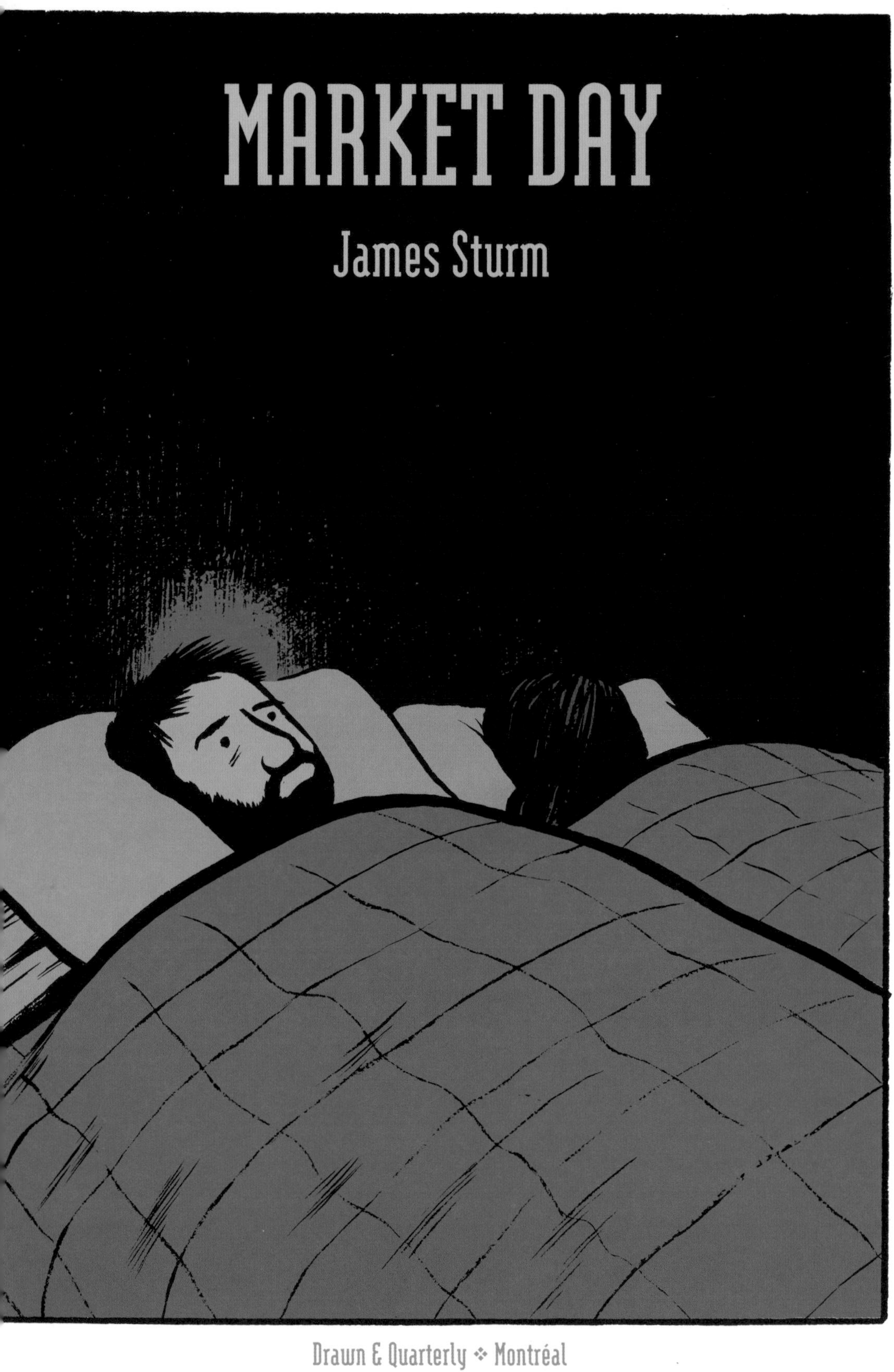

Drawn & Quarterly ❖ Montréal

may be reproduced in any form without written permission from James Sturm or Drawn & Quarterly. Production Assistance: Joe Lambert. Drawn & Quarterly, Post Office Box 48056, Montreal, Quebec, Canada H2V 4S8; www.drawnandquarterly.com; First hardcover edition: March 2010. 10 9 8 7 6 5 4 3 2 1; Printed in China. Library and Archives Canada Cataloguing in Publication; Sturm, James, 1965- ; Market day / James Sturm. ISBN 978-1-897299-97-5; I. Title. PN6727.S78M37 2010   741.5'973   C2009-906771-4; Distributed in the USA by Farrar, Straus & Giroux, 18 West 18th Street, New York, NY 10011; Orders: 888.330.8477; Distributed in Canada by Raincoast Books, 9050 Shaughnessy Street, Vancouver, BC V6P 6E5; Orders: 800.663.5714; Distributed in the United Kingdom by Publishers Group U.K., 8 The Arena, Mollison Avenue, Enfield Middlesex EN3 7NL; Orders: 0208 8040400

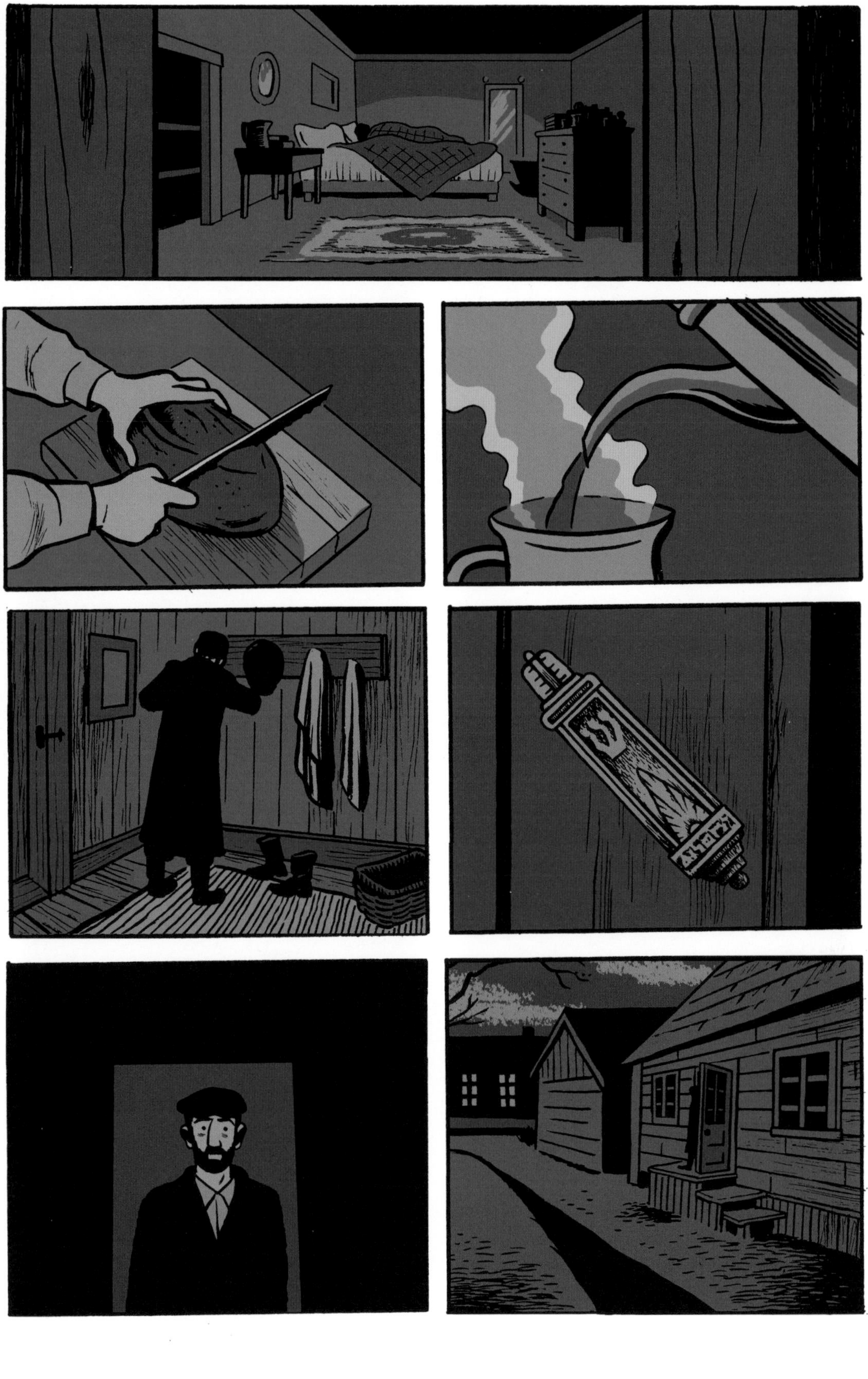

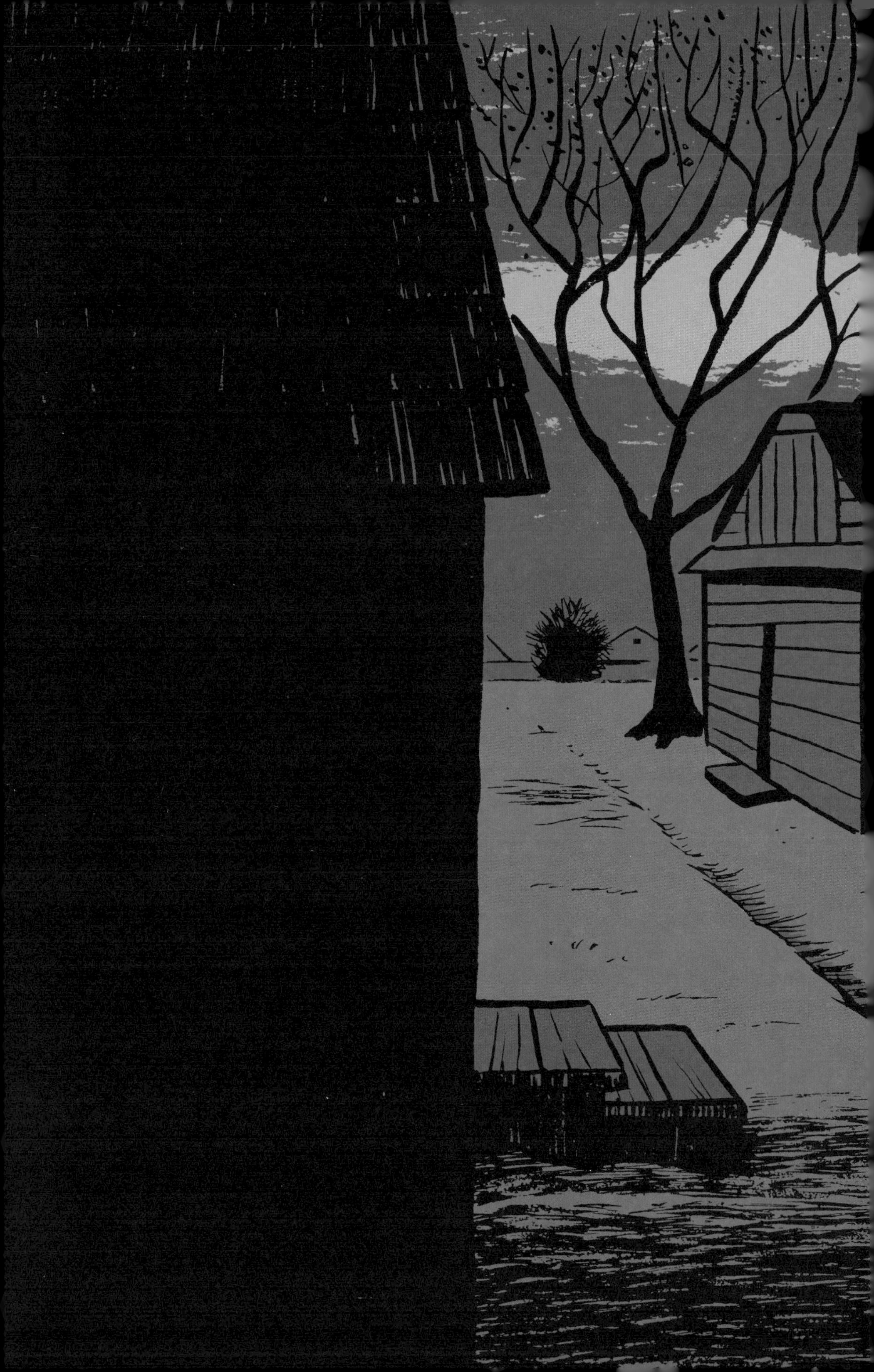

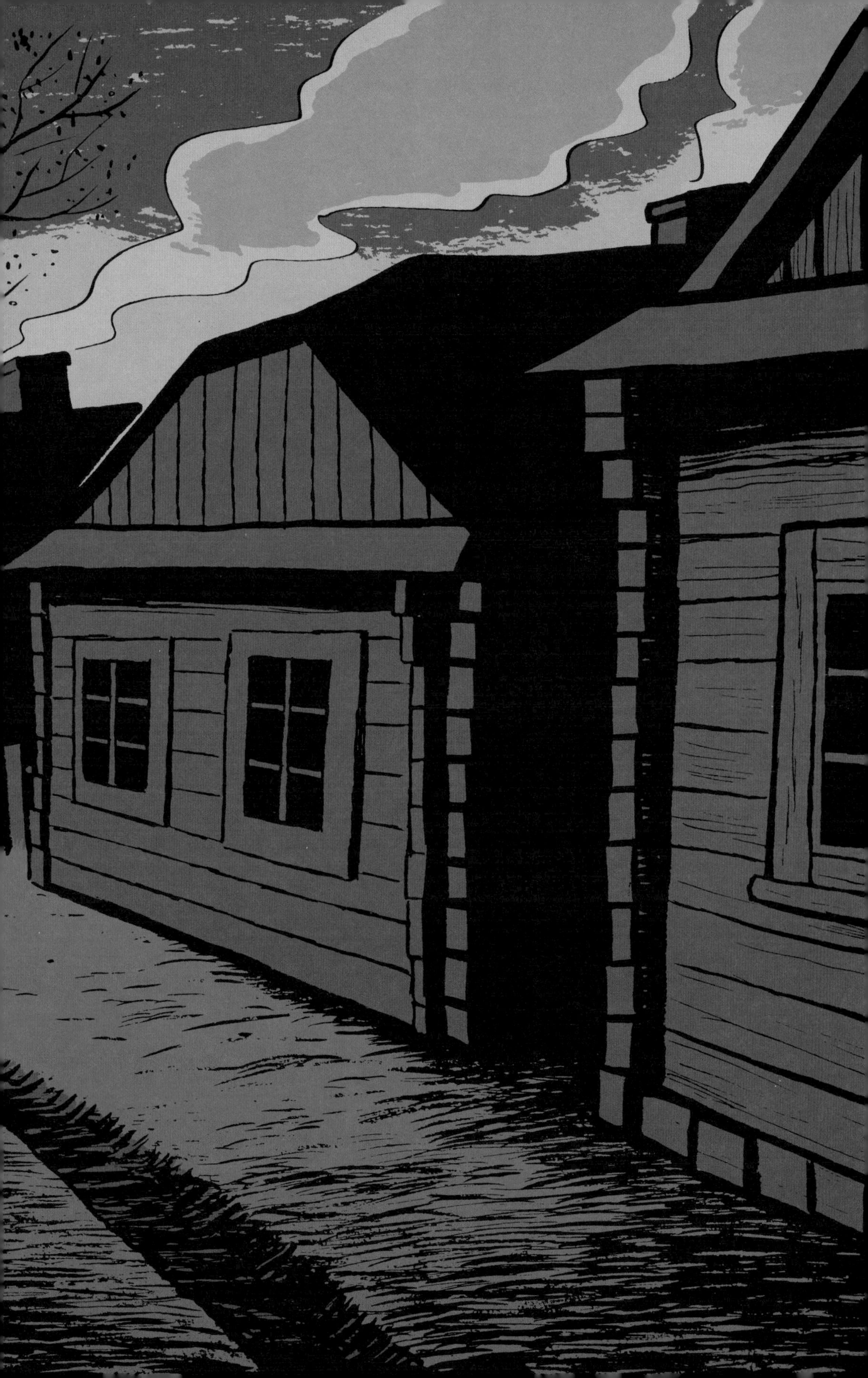

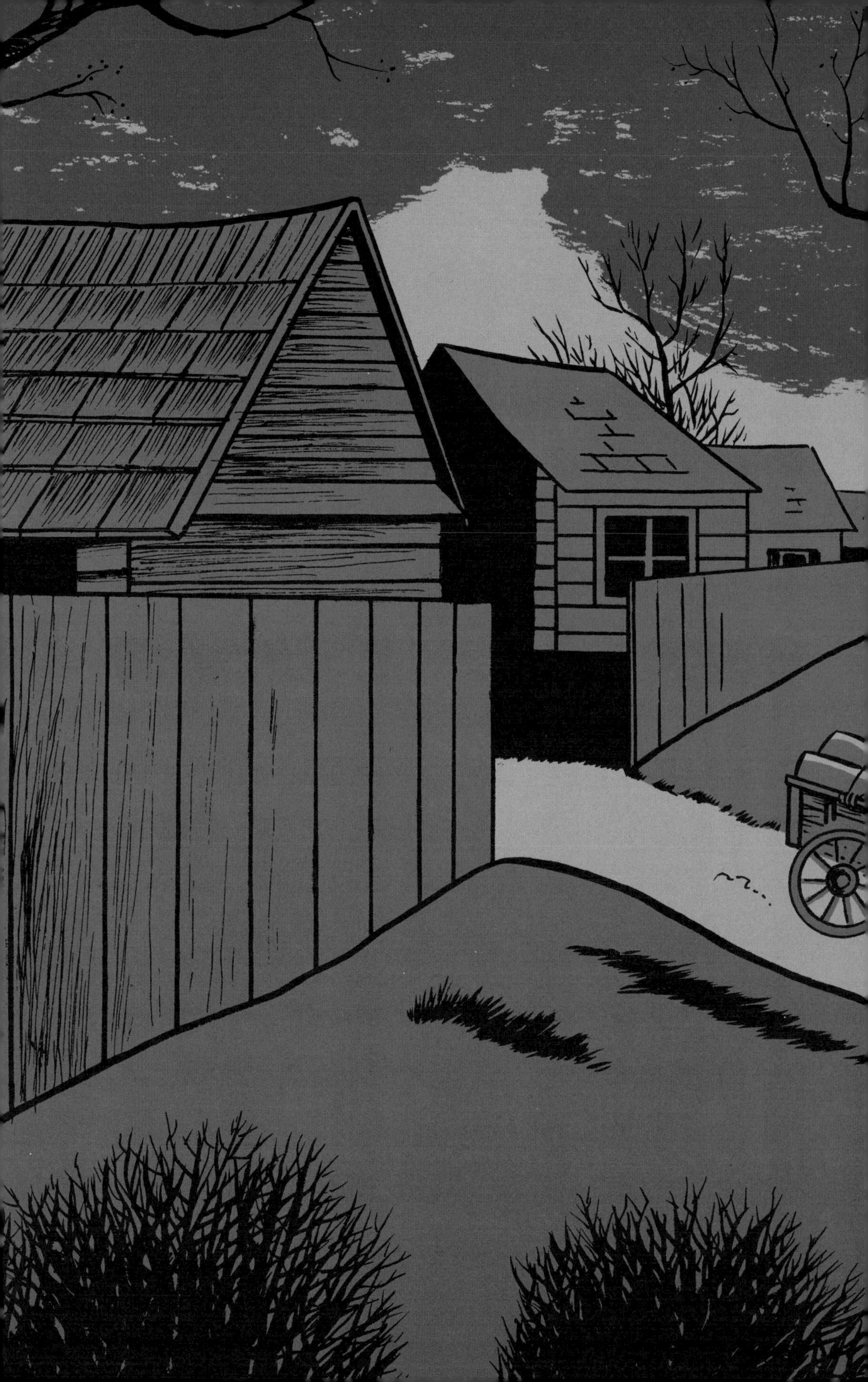

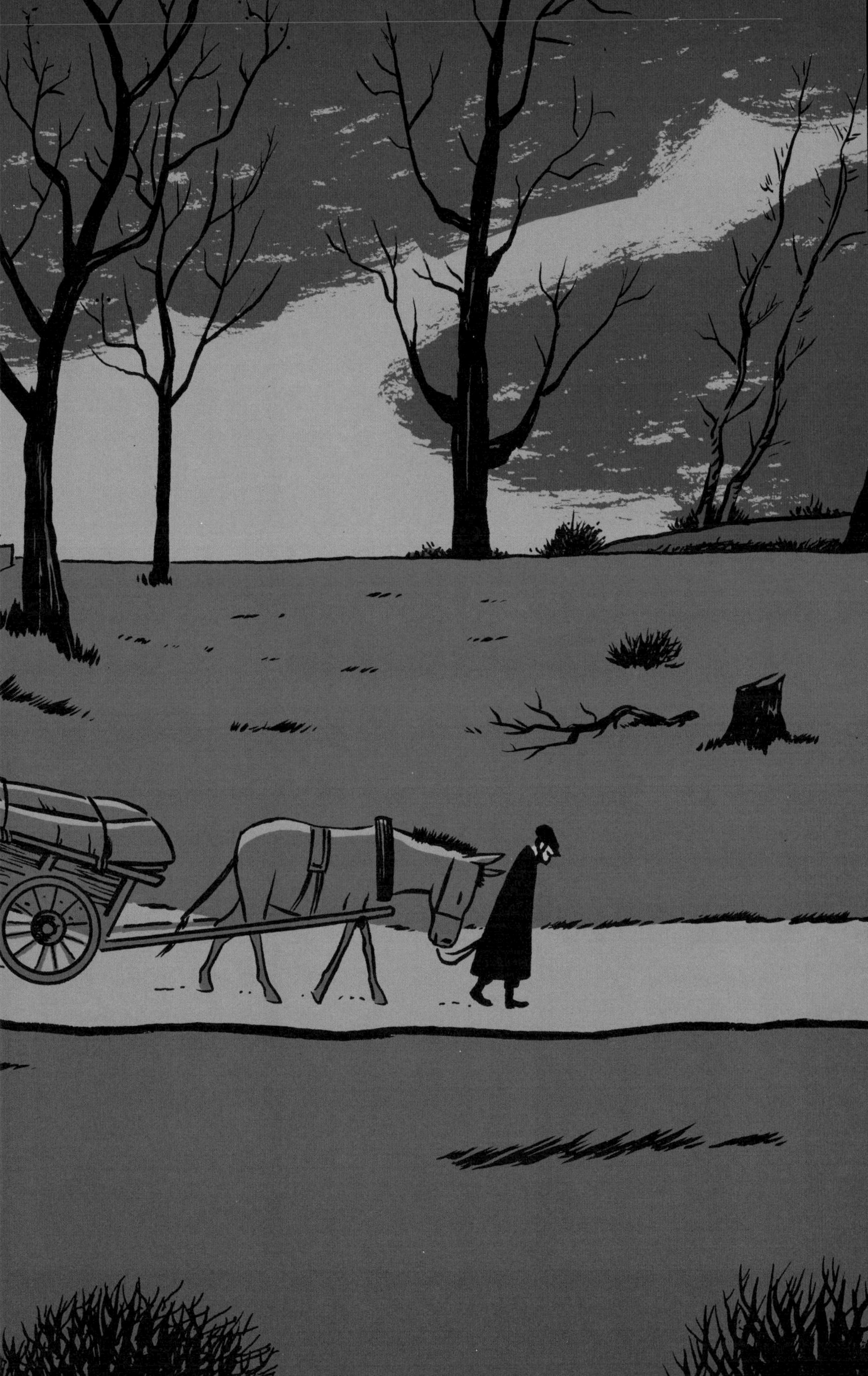

I NEVER SLEEP WELL THE NIGHT BEFORE MARKET DAY.
USUALLY IT IS DUE TO EXCITEMENT BUT
TONIGHT IT IS DUE TO DREAD.

MY WIFE WILL NOT
ACCOMPANY ME
THIS TIME.

RACHEL IS EIGHT MONTHS
PREGNANT WITH OUR
FIRST CHILD.

IT IS NOT MY INTENTION
TO DRAIN THE JOY
FROM ONE OF LIFE'S
TRUE MIRACLES...

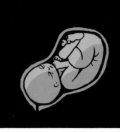

BUT MY THOUGHTS
INCREASINGLY DWELL
ON DEATH.

RECENTLY RACHEL'S
TWIN SISTER LOST
HER CHILD AT BIRTH.

HOURS AGO I CONVINCED
MYSELF THAT IF I
WENT TO THE MARKET
I WOULD NEVER SEE
RACHEL AGAIN.

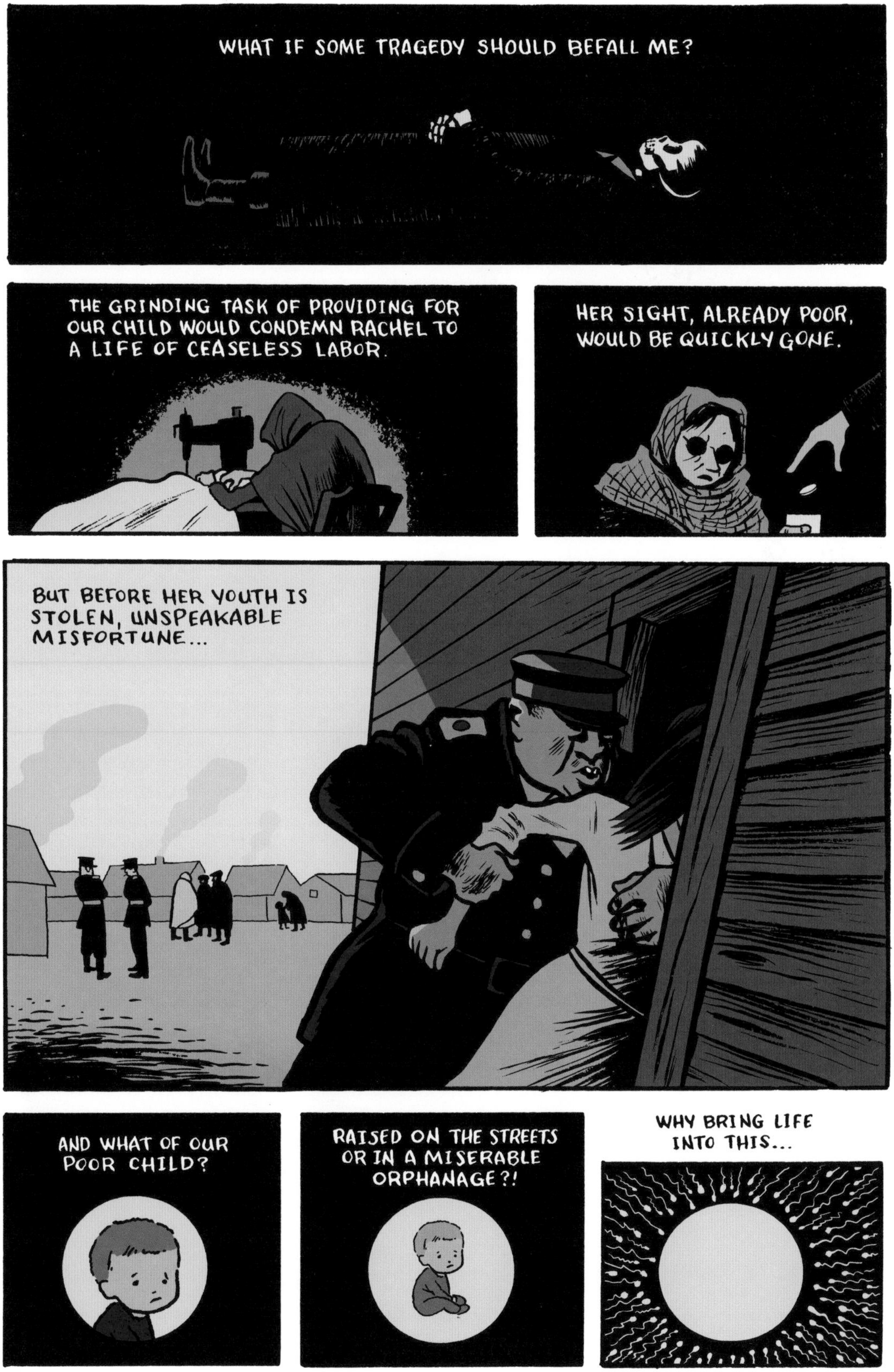
WHAT IF SOME TRAGEDY SHOULD BEFALL ME?
THE GRINDING TASK OF PROVIDING FOR OUR CHILD WOULD CONDEMN RACHEL TO A LIFE OF CEASELESS LABOR.
HER SIGHT, ALREADY POOR, WOULD BE QUICKLY GONE.
BUT BEFORE HER YOUTH IS STOLEN, UNSPEAKABLE MISFORTUNE...
AND WHAT OF OUR POOR CHILD?
RAISED ON THE STREETS OR IN A MISERABLE ORPHANAGE?!
WHY BRING LIFE INTO THIS...

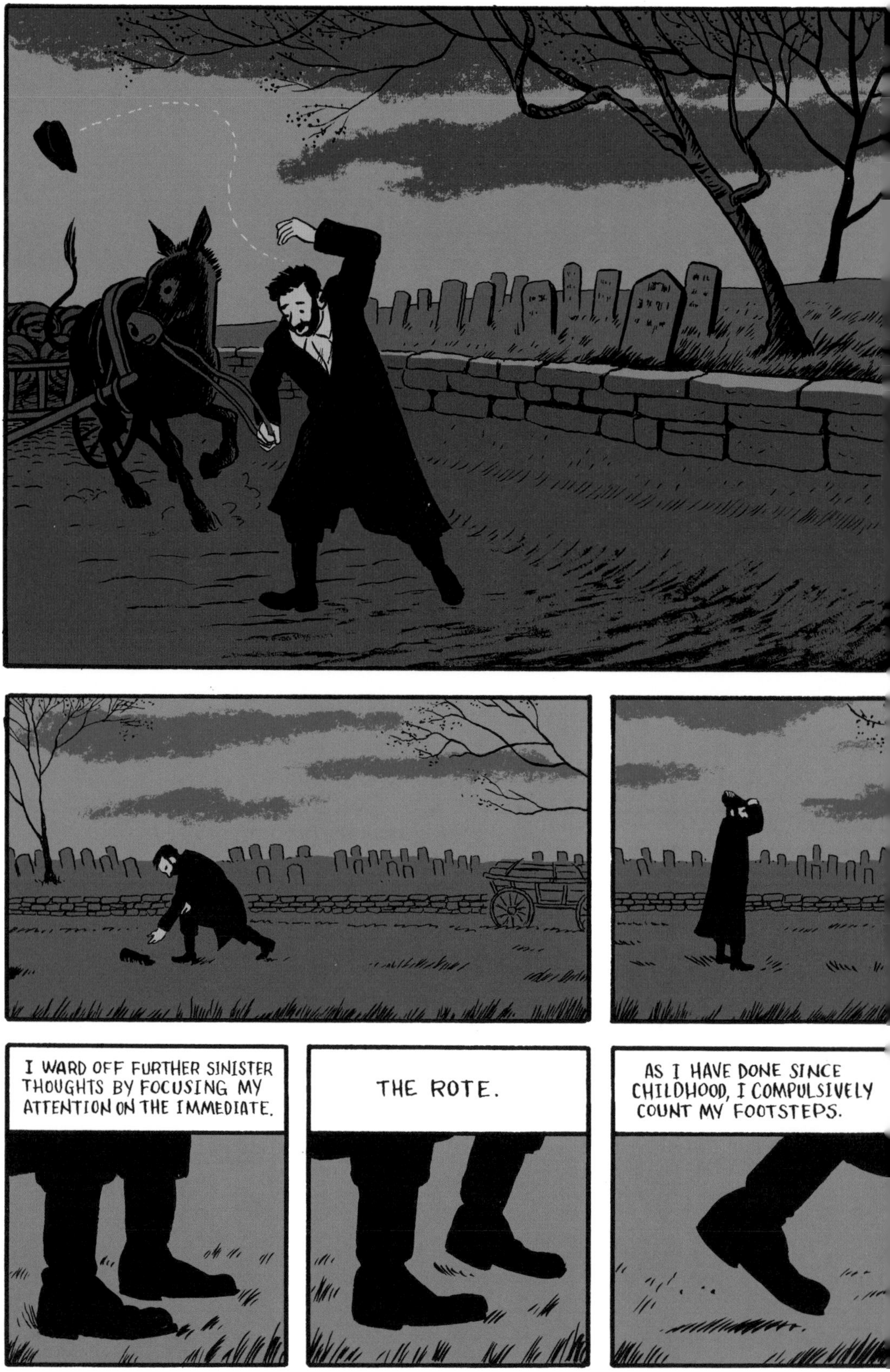
I WARD OFF FURTHER SINISTER THOUGHTS BY FOCUSING MY ATTENTION ON THE IMMEDIATE.
THE ROTE.
AS I HAVE DONE SINCE CHILDHOOD, I COMPULSIVELY COUNT MY FOOTSTEPS.

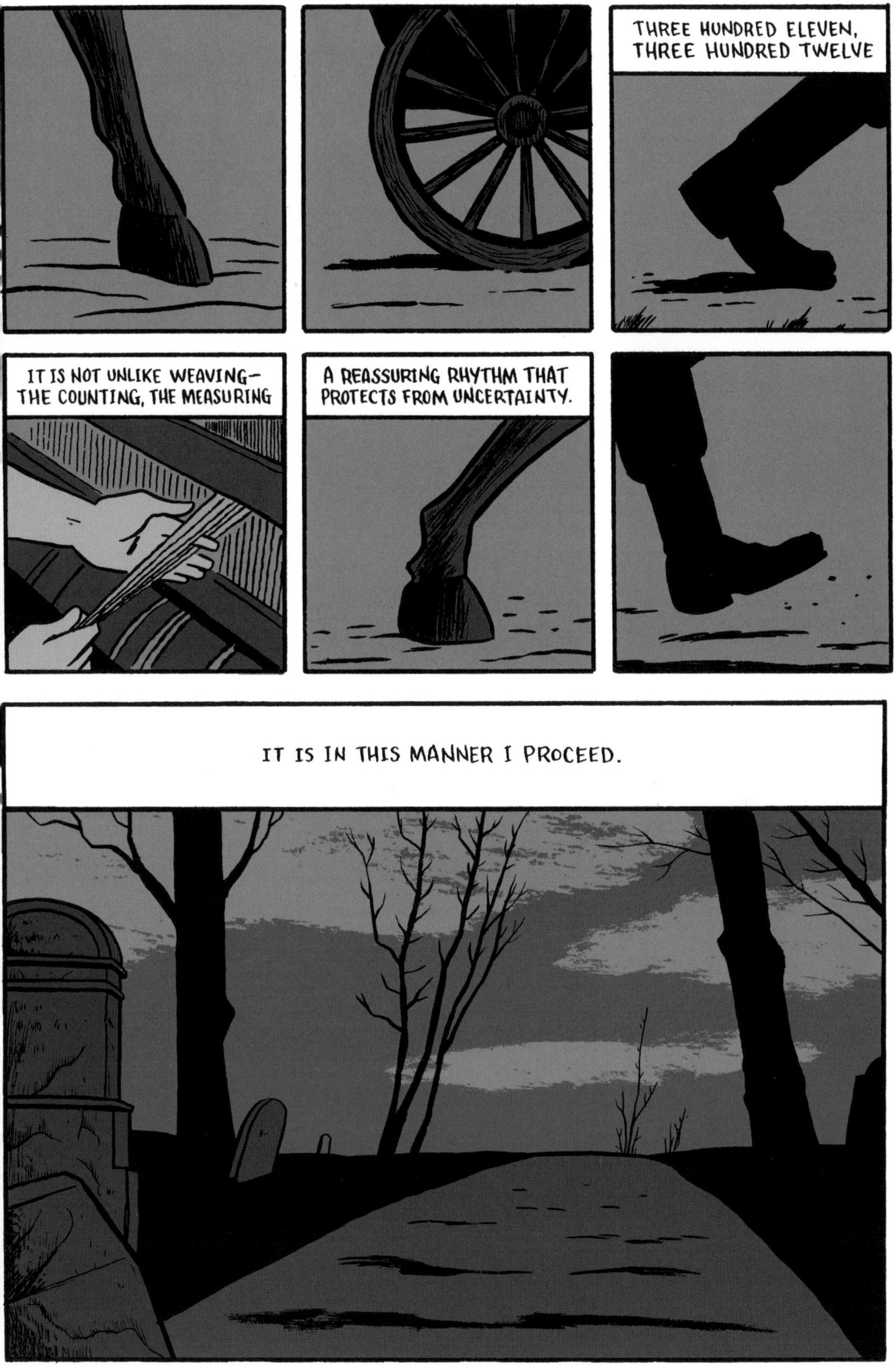
THREE HUNDRED ELEVEN, THREE HUNDRED TWELVE
IT IS NOT UNLIKE WEAVING— THE COUNTING, THE MEASURING
A REASSURING RHYTHM THAT PROTECTS FROM UNCERTAINTY.
IT IS IN THIS MANNER I PROCEED.

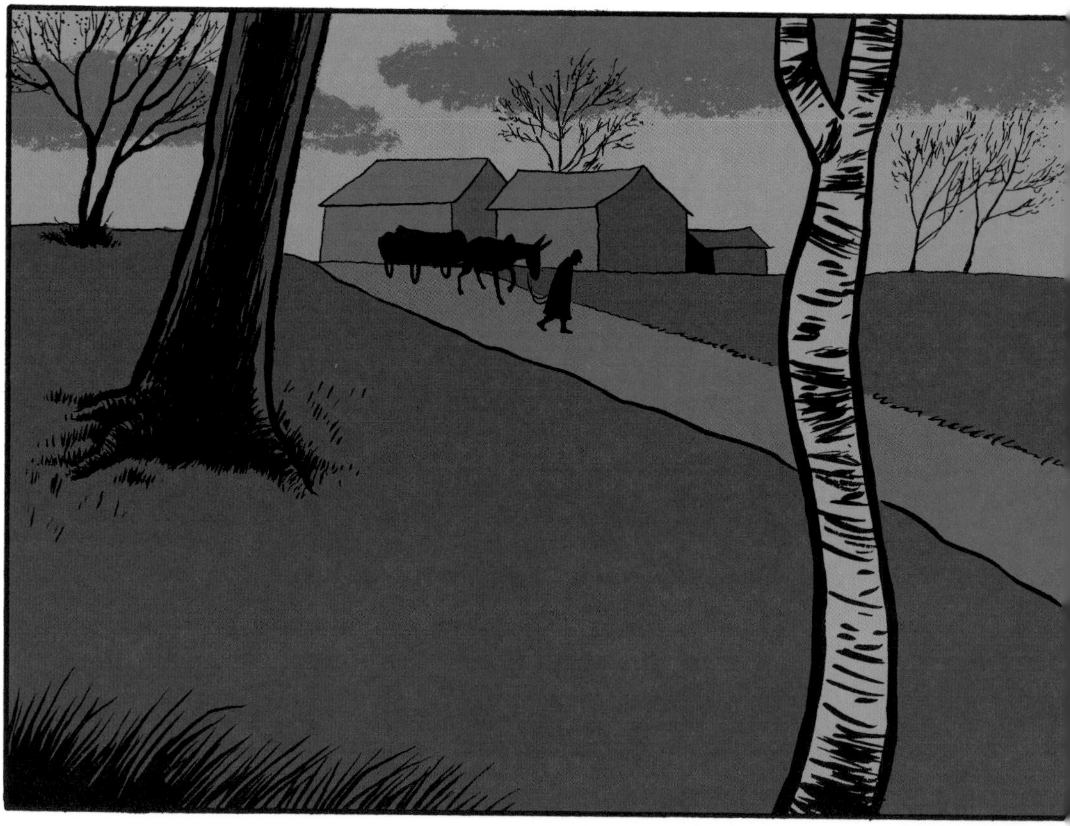

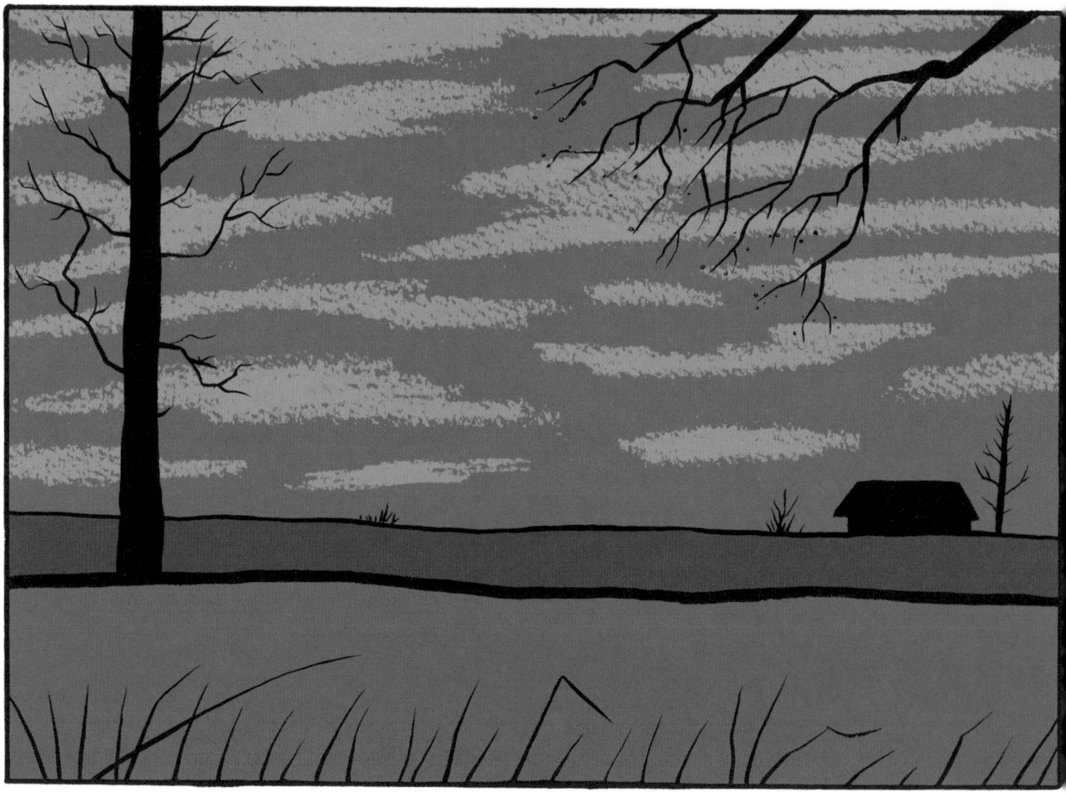

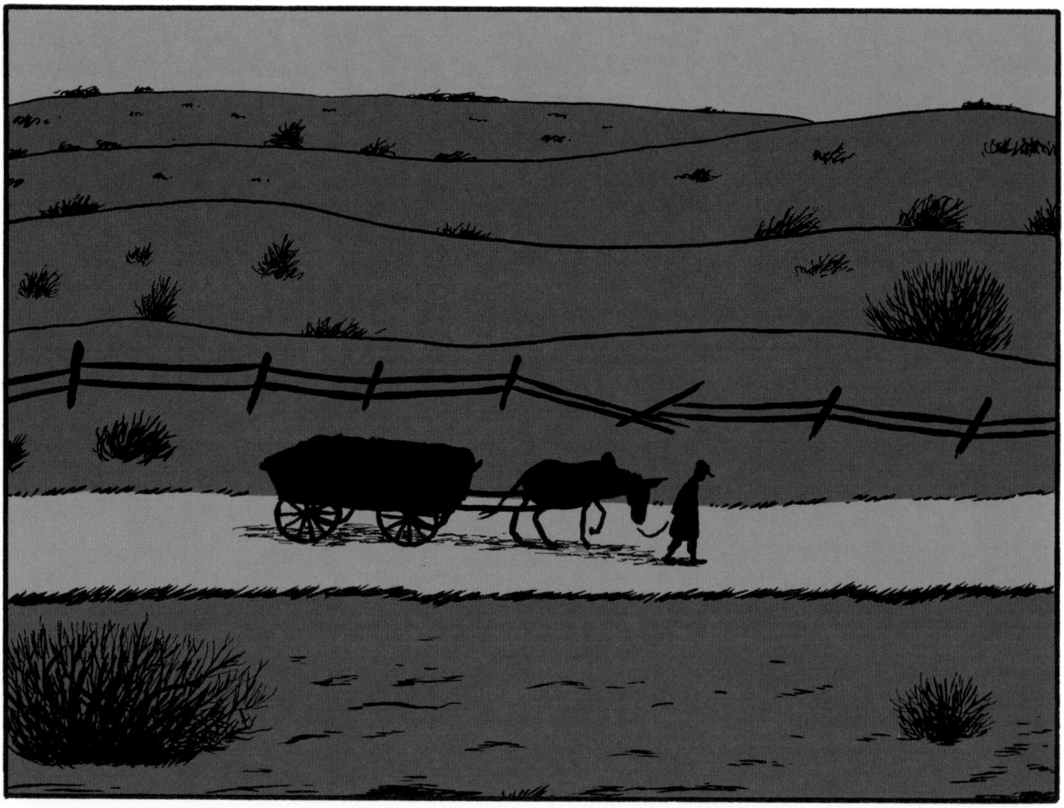
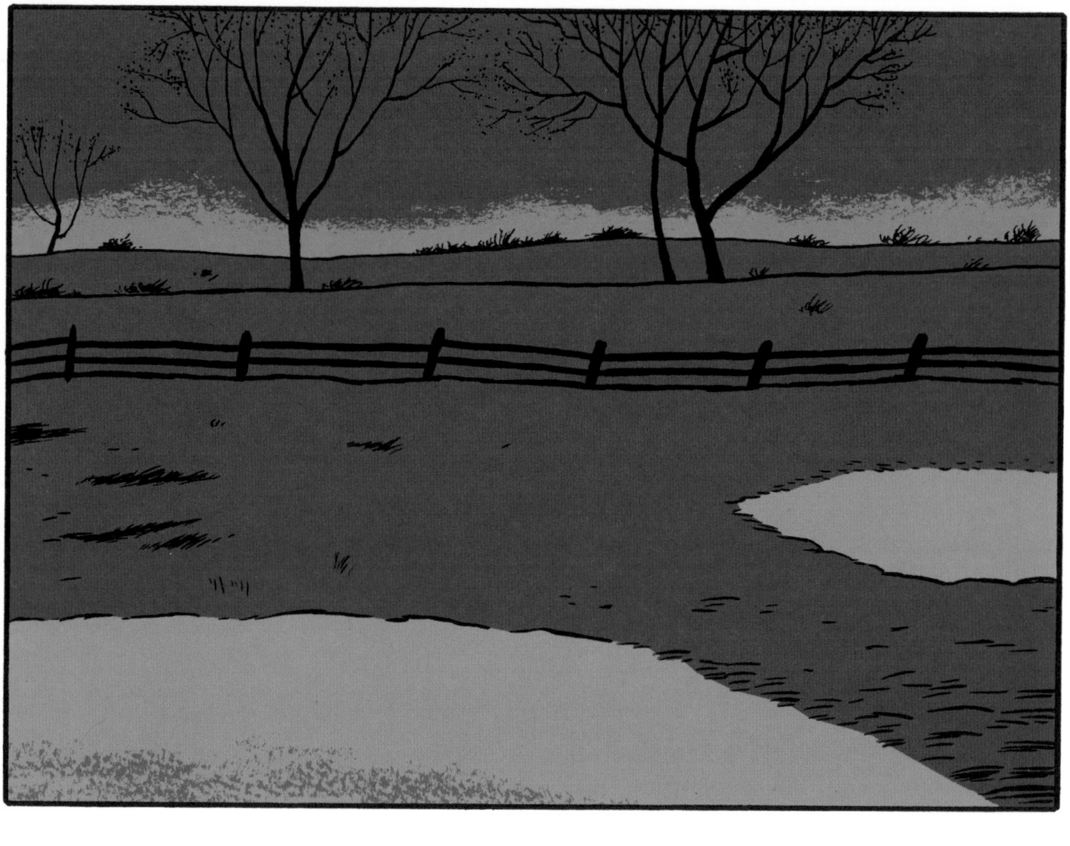

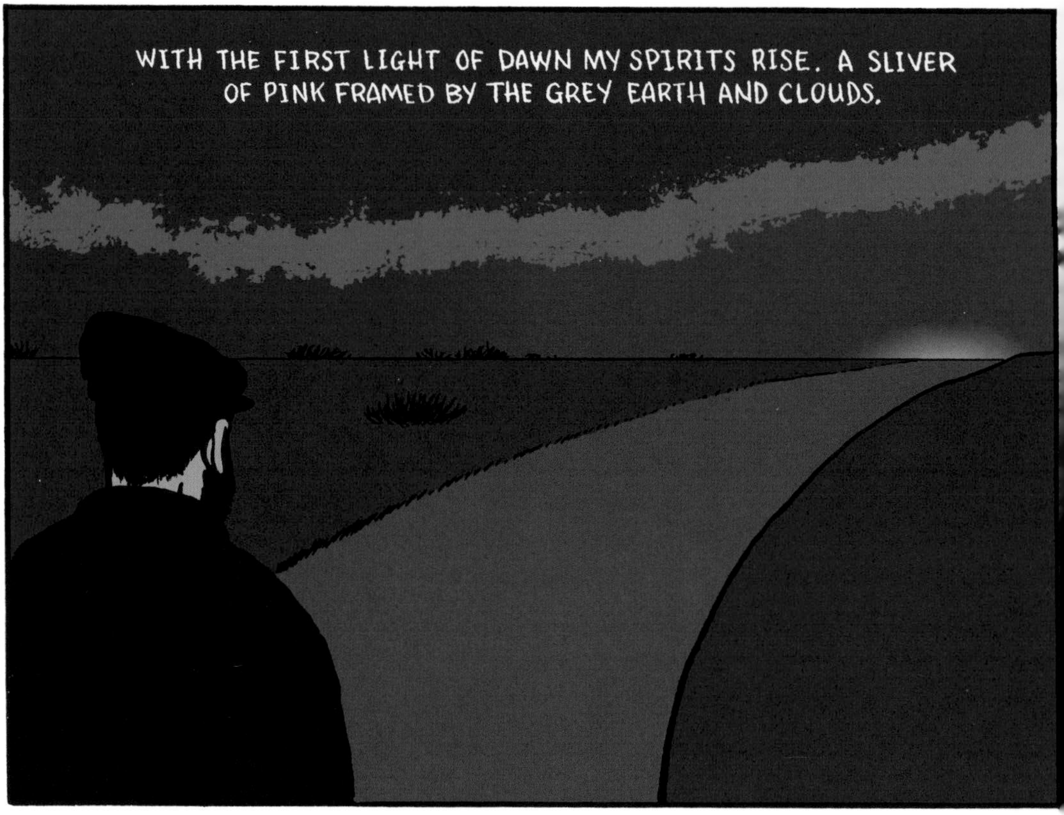
WITH THE FIRST LIGHT OF DAWN MY SPIRITS RISE. A SLIVER OF PINK FRAMED BY THE GREY EARTH AND CLOUDS.

I IMMEDIATELY TRY TO THINK OF HOW I COULD REFLECT THIS MOMENT IN A RUG. A SMALL STREAK OF COLOR SLICING THROUGH A LARGE BLOCK OF GREY.

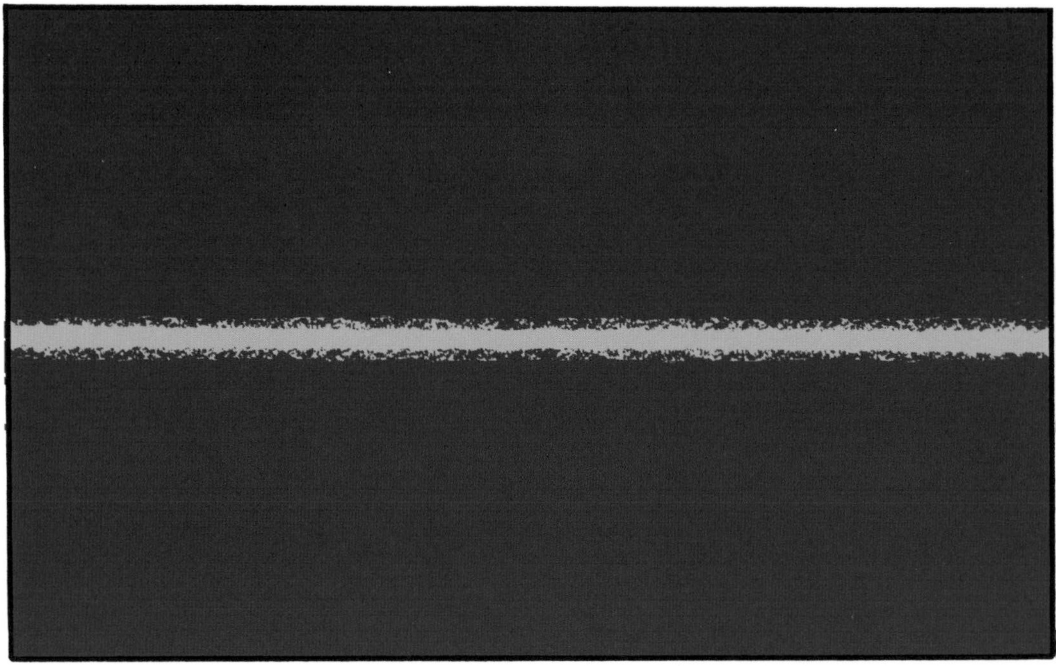

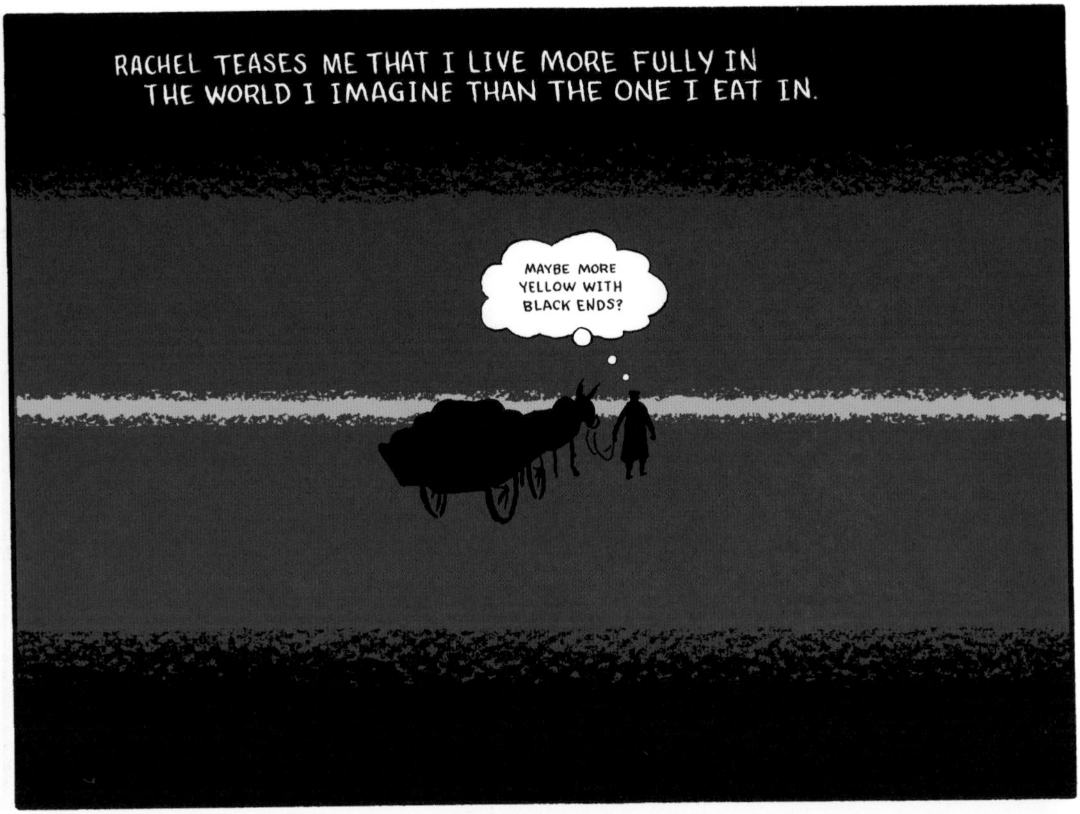
RACHEL TEASES ME THAT I LIVE MORE FULLY IN THE WORLD I IMAGINE THAN THE ONE I EAT IN.
MAYBE MORE YELLOW WITH BLACK ENDS?

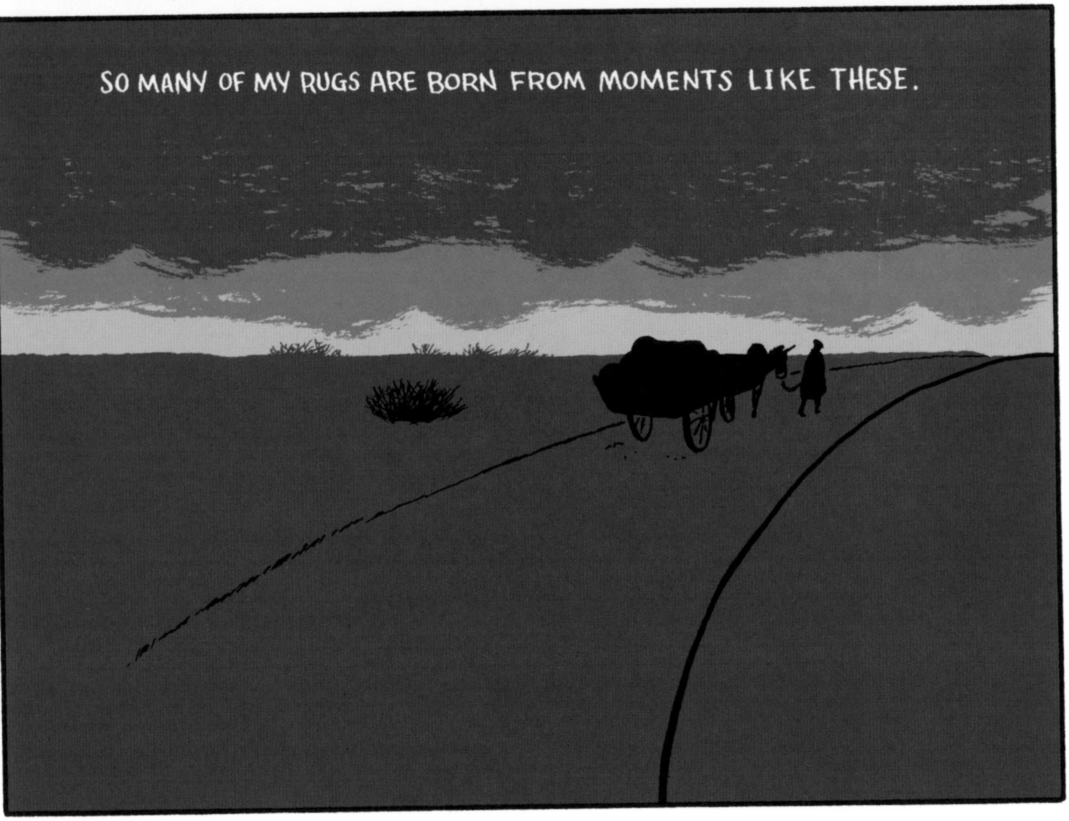
SO MANY OF MY RUGS ARE BORN FROM MOMENTS LIKE THESE.

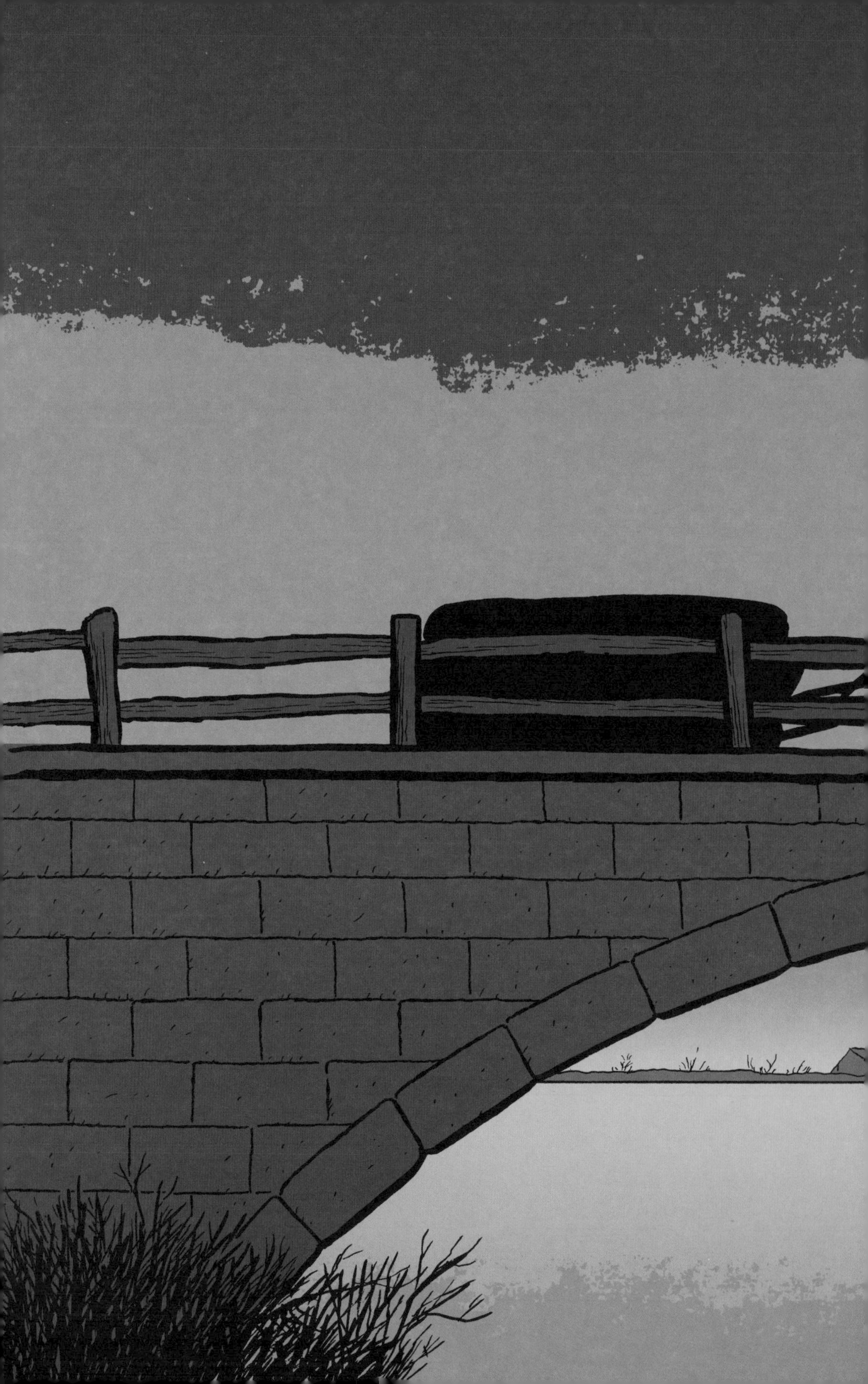

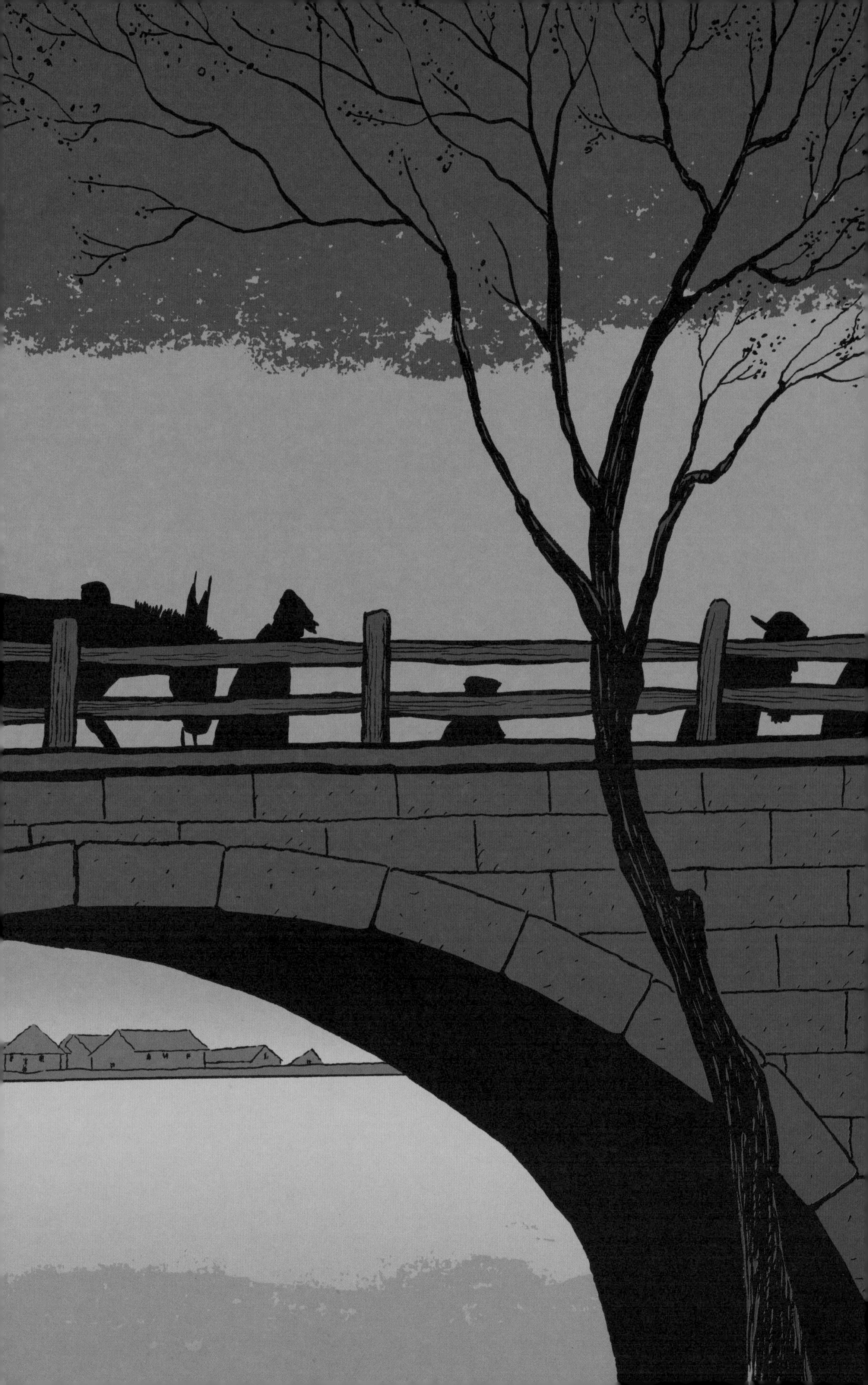

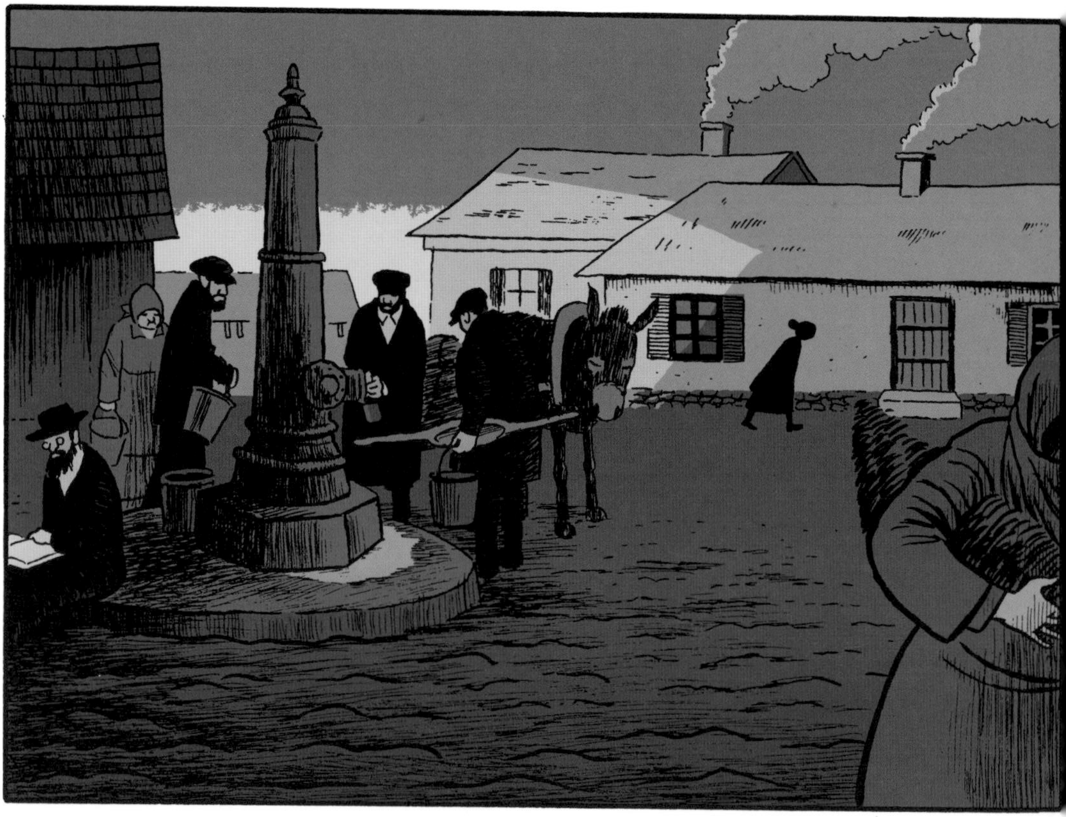

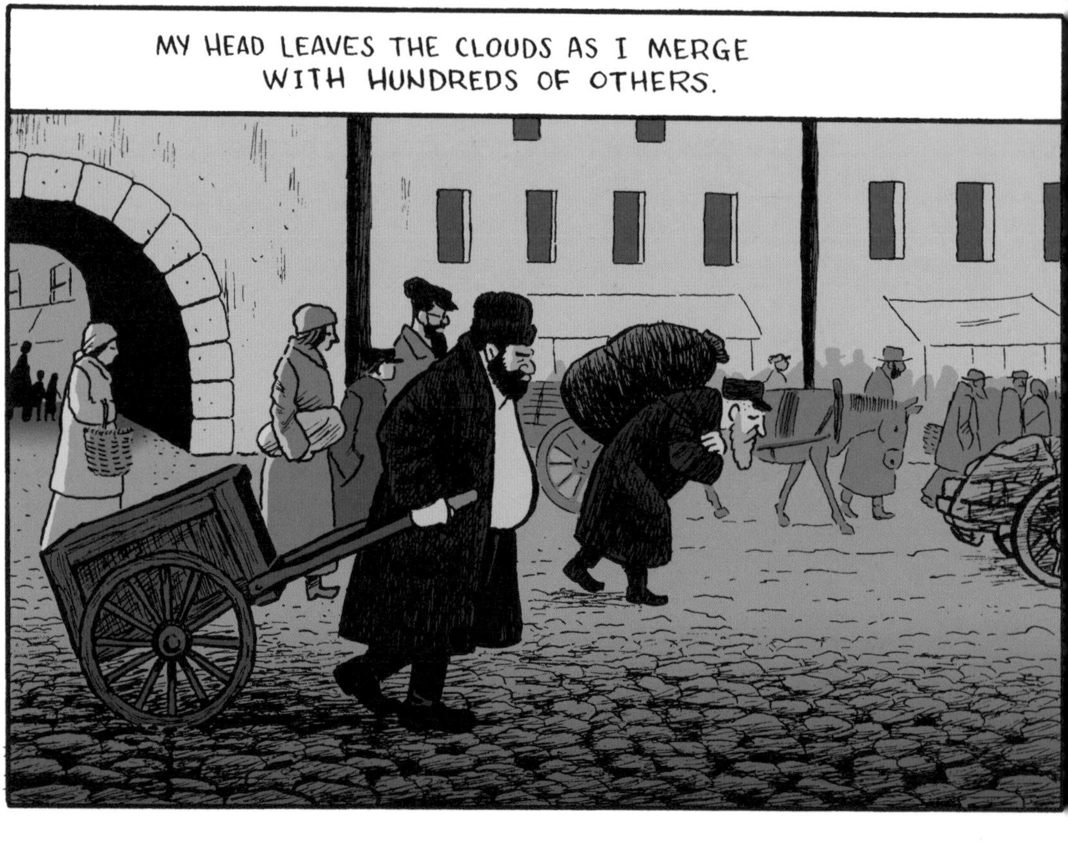
MY HEAD LEAVES THE CLOUDS AS I MERGE WITH HUNDREDS OF OTHERS.

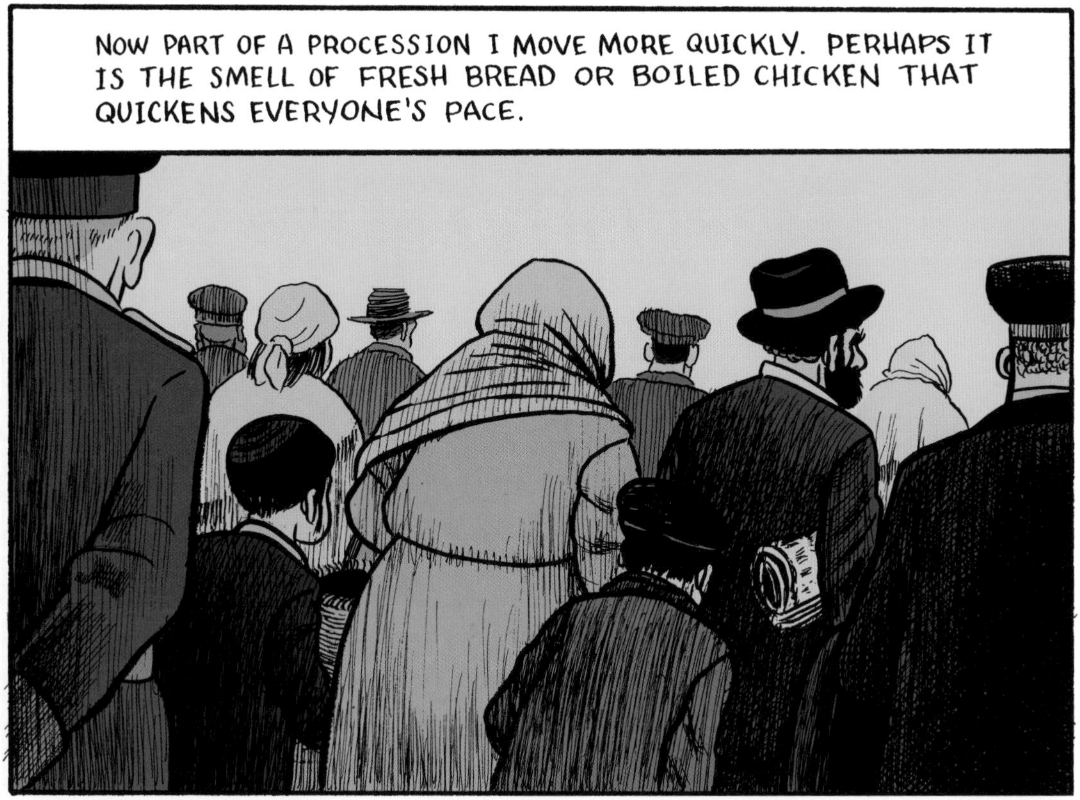
NOW PART OF A PROCESSION I MOVE MORE QUICKLY. PERHAPS IT IS THE SMELL OF FRESH BREAD OR BOILED CHICKEN THAT QUICKENS EVERYONE'S PACE.

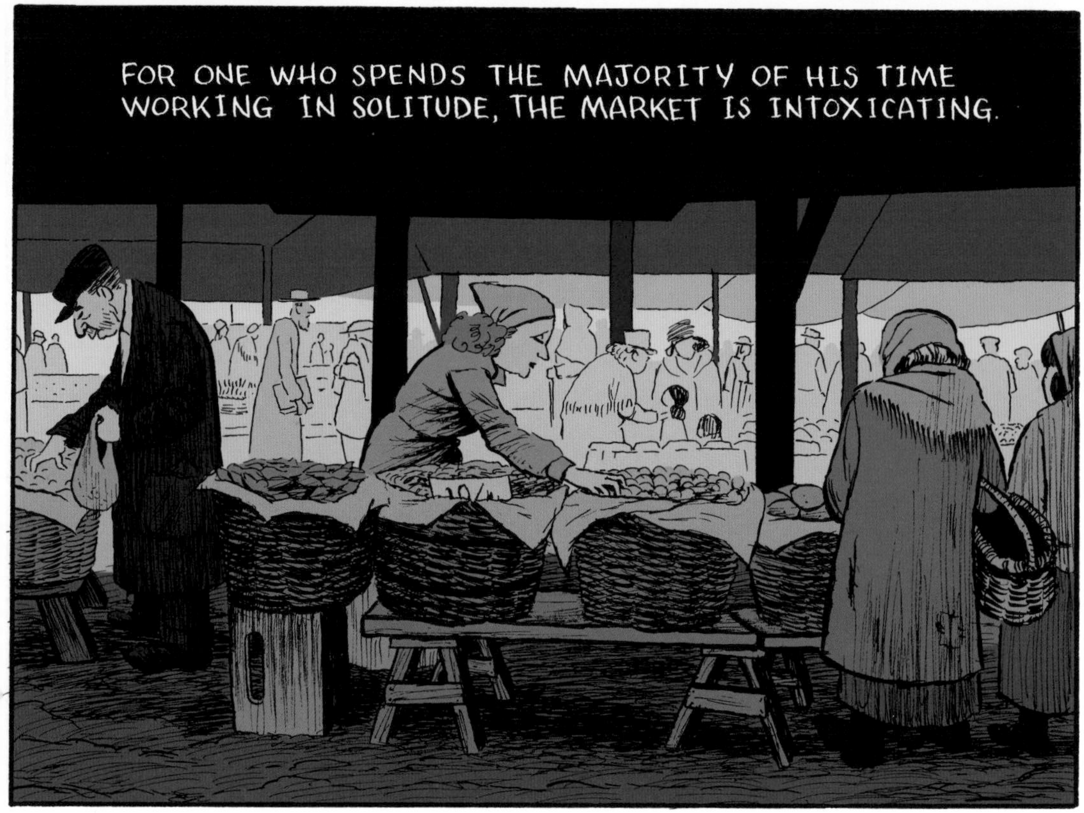
FOR ONE WHO SPENDS THE MAJORITY OF HIS TIME WORKING IN SOLITUDE, THE MARKET IS INTOXICATING.

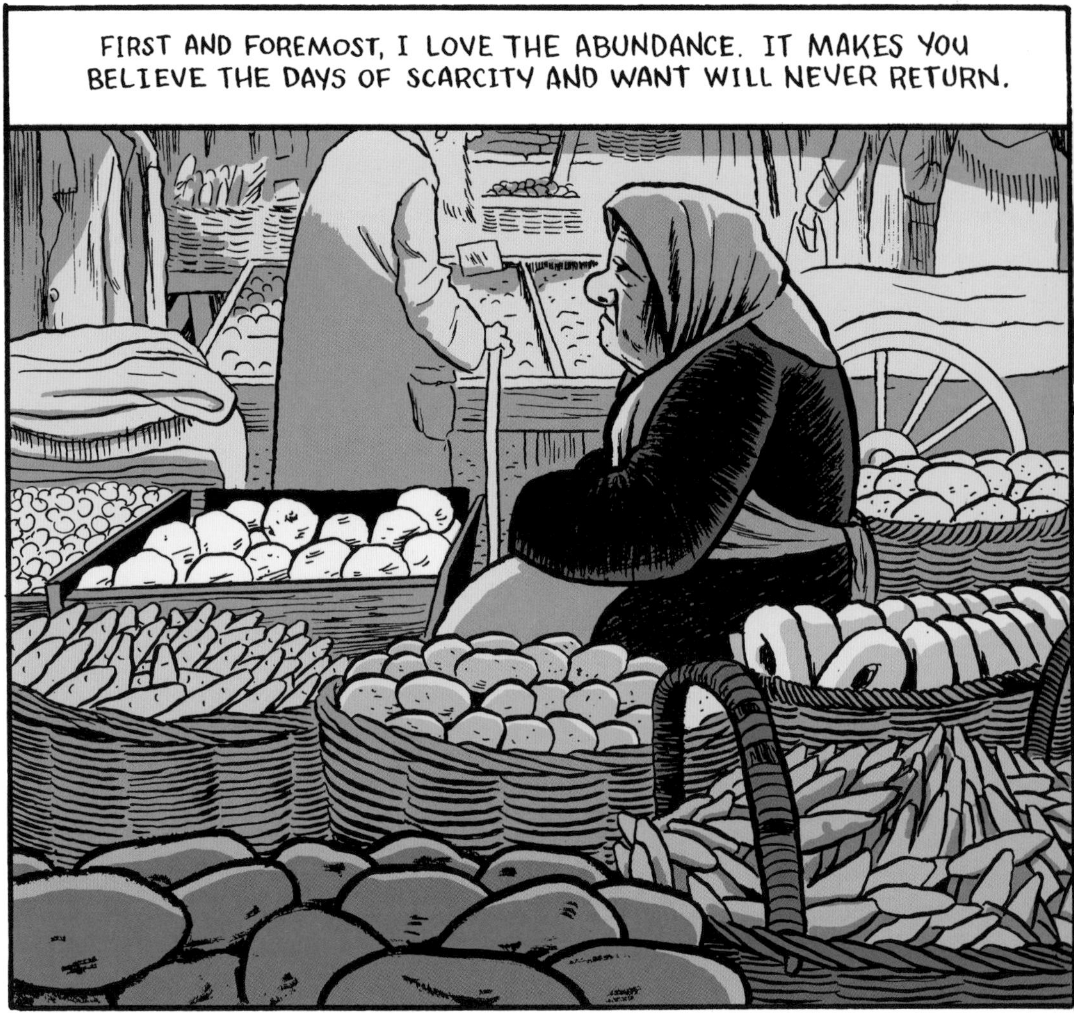
FIRST AND FOREMOST, I LOVE THE ABUNDANCE. IT MAKES YOU BELIEVE THE DAYS OF SCARCITY AND WANT WILL NEVER RETURN.

I LOVE THE CHILDREN, OBLIVIOUS TO EVERYTHING BUT THEIR OWN FUN...

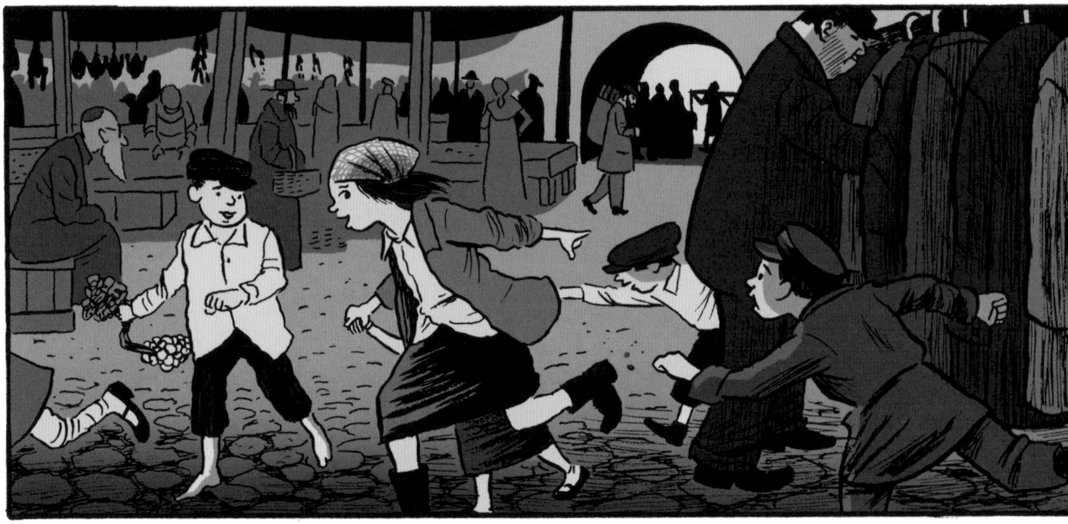

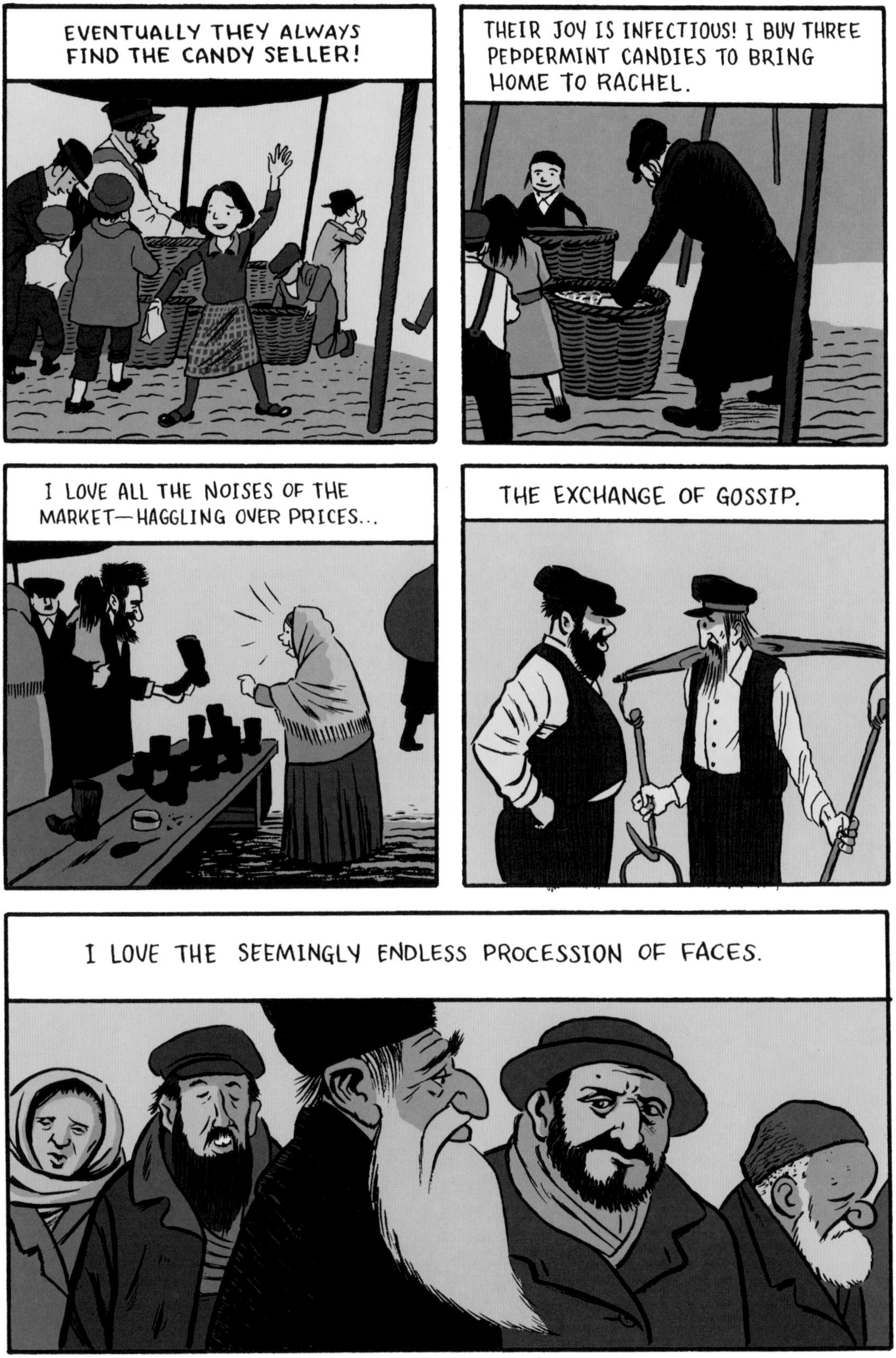
EVENTUALLY THEY ALWAYS FIND THE CANDY SELLER!
THEIR JOY IS INFECTIOUS! I BUY THREE PEPPERMINT CANDIES TO BRING HOME TO RACHEL.
I LOVE ALL THE NOISES OF THE MARKET—HAGGLING OVER PRICES...
THE EXCHANGE OF GOSSIP.
I LOVE THE SEEMINGLY ENDLESS PROCESSION OF FACES.

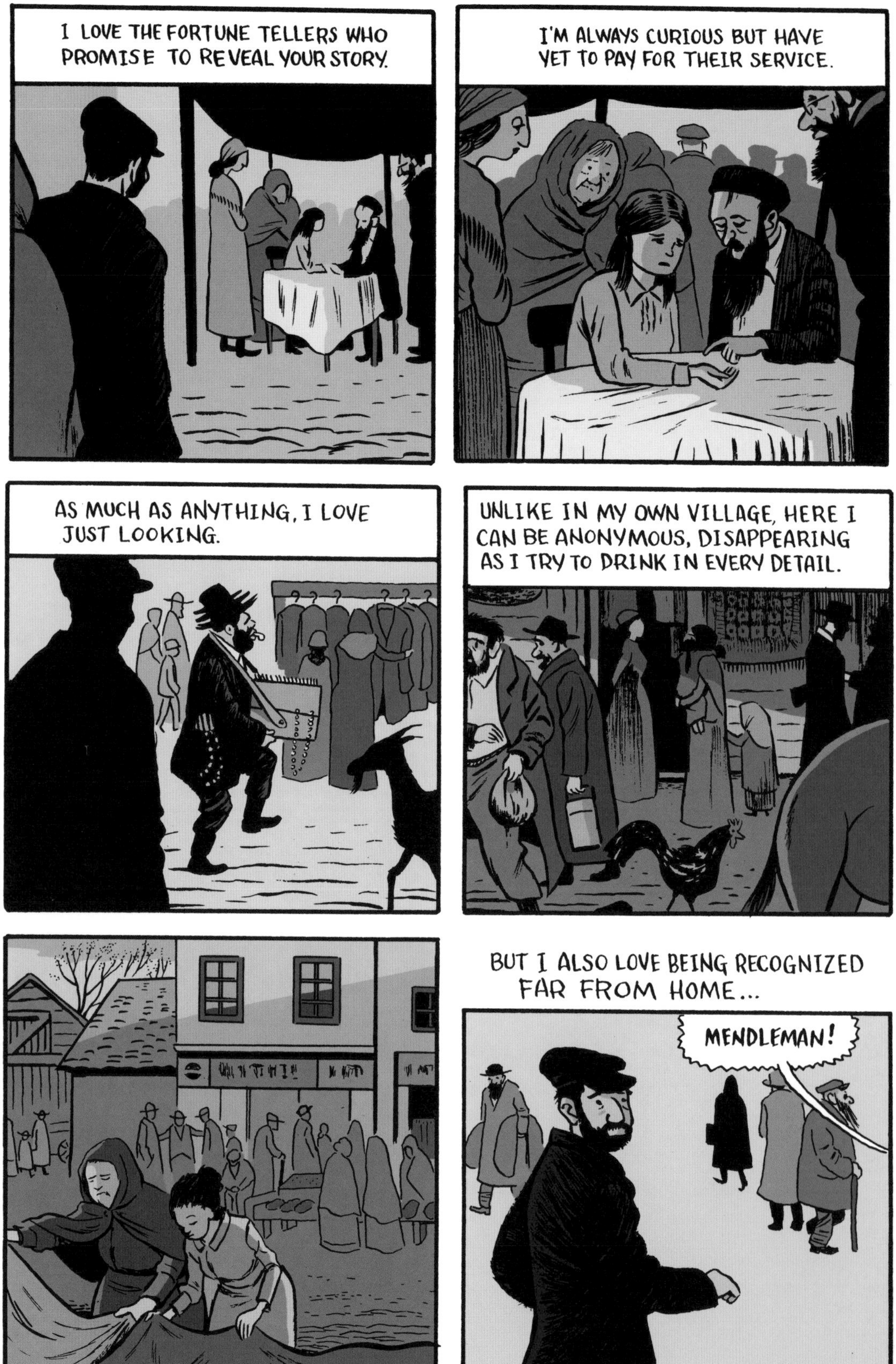
I LOVE THE FORTUNE TELLERS WHO PROMISE TO REVEAL YOUR STORY.
I'M ALWAYS CURIOUS BUT HAVE YET TO PAY FOR THEIR SERVICE.
AS MUCH AS ANYTHING, I LOVE JUST LOOKING.
UNLIKE IN MY OWN VILLAGE, HERE I CAN BE ANONYMOUS, DISAPPEARING AS I TRY TO DRINK IN EVERY DETAIL.
BUT I ALSO LOVE BEING RECOGNIZED FAR FROM HOME...
MENDLEMAN!

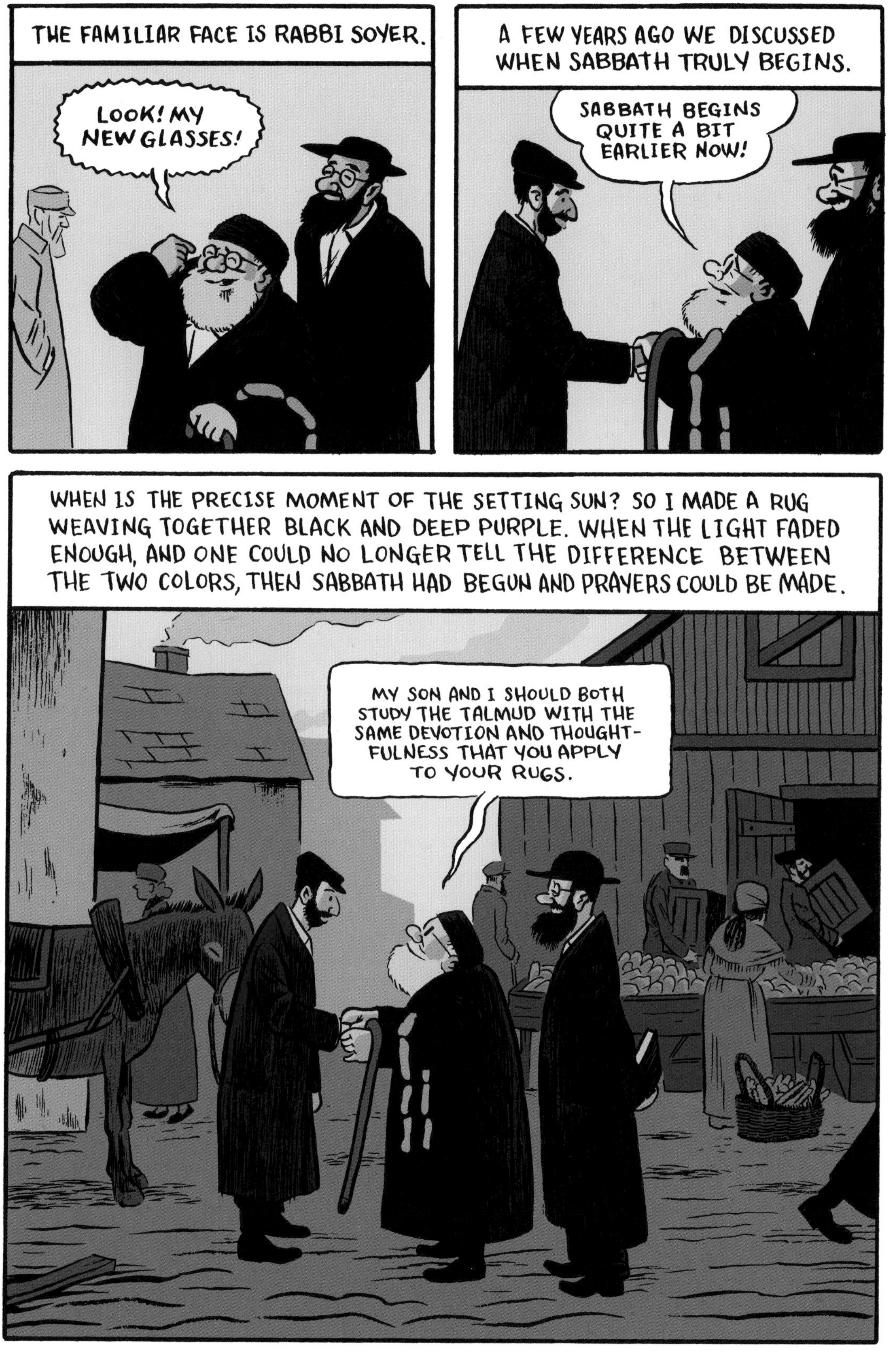
THE FAMILIAR FACE IS RABBI SOYER.
LOOK! MY NEW GLASSES!
A FEW YEARS AGO WE DISCUSSED WHEN SABBATH TRULY BEGINS.
SABBATH BEGINS QUITE A BIT EARLIER NOW!
WHEN IS THE PRECISE MOMENT OF THE SETTING SUN? SO I MADE A RUG WEAVING TOGETHER BLACK AND DEEP PURPLE. WHEN THE LIGHT FADED ENOUGH, AND ONE COULD NO LONGER TELL THE DIFFERENCE BETWEEN THE TWO COLORS, THEN SABBATH HAD BEGUN AND PRAYERS COULD BE MADE.
MY SON AND I SHOULD BOTH STUDY THE TALMUD WITH THE SAME DEVOTION AND THOUGHTFULNESS THAT YOU APPLY TO YOUR RUGS.

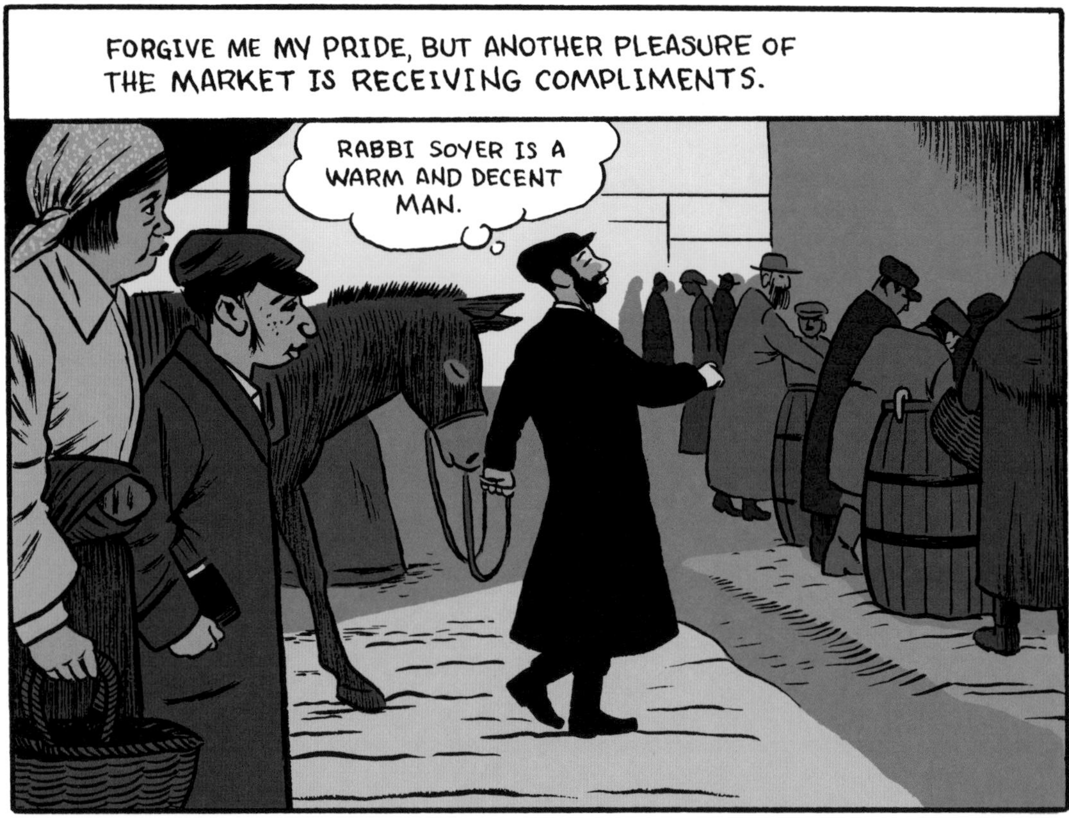
FORGIVE ME MY PRIDE, BUT ANOTHER PLEASURE OF THE MARKET IS RECEIVING COMPLIMENTS.
RABBI SOYER IS A WARM AND DECENT MAN.

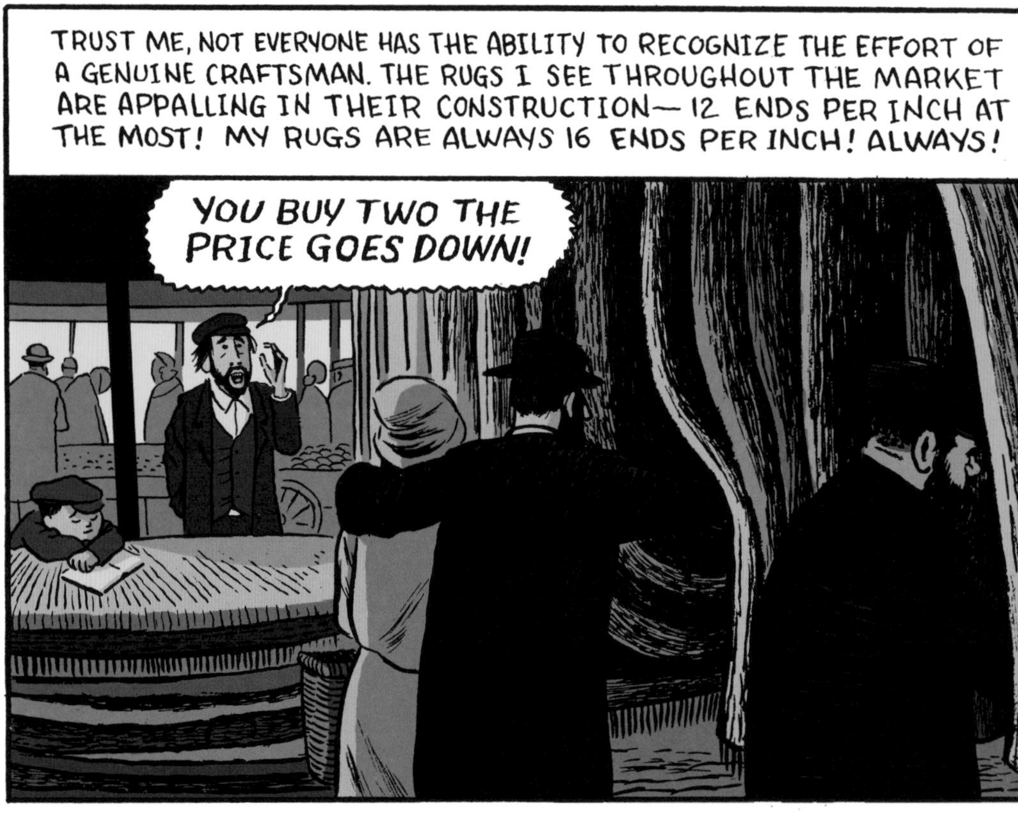
TRUST ME, NOT EVERYONE HAS THE ABILITY TO RECOGNIZE THE EFFORT OF A GENUINE CRAFTSMAN. THE RUGS I SEE THROUGHOUT THE MARKET ARE APPALLING IN THEIR CONSTRUCTION— 12 ENDS PER INCH AT THE MOST! MY RUGS ARE ALWAYS 16 ENDS PER INCH! ALWAYS!
YOU BUY TWO THE PRICE GOES DOWN!

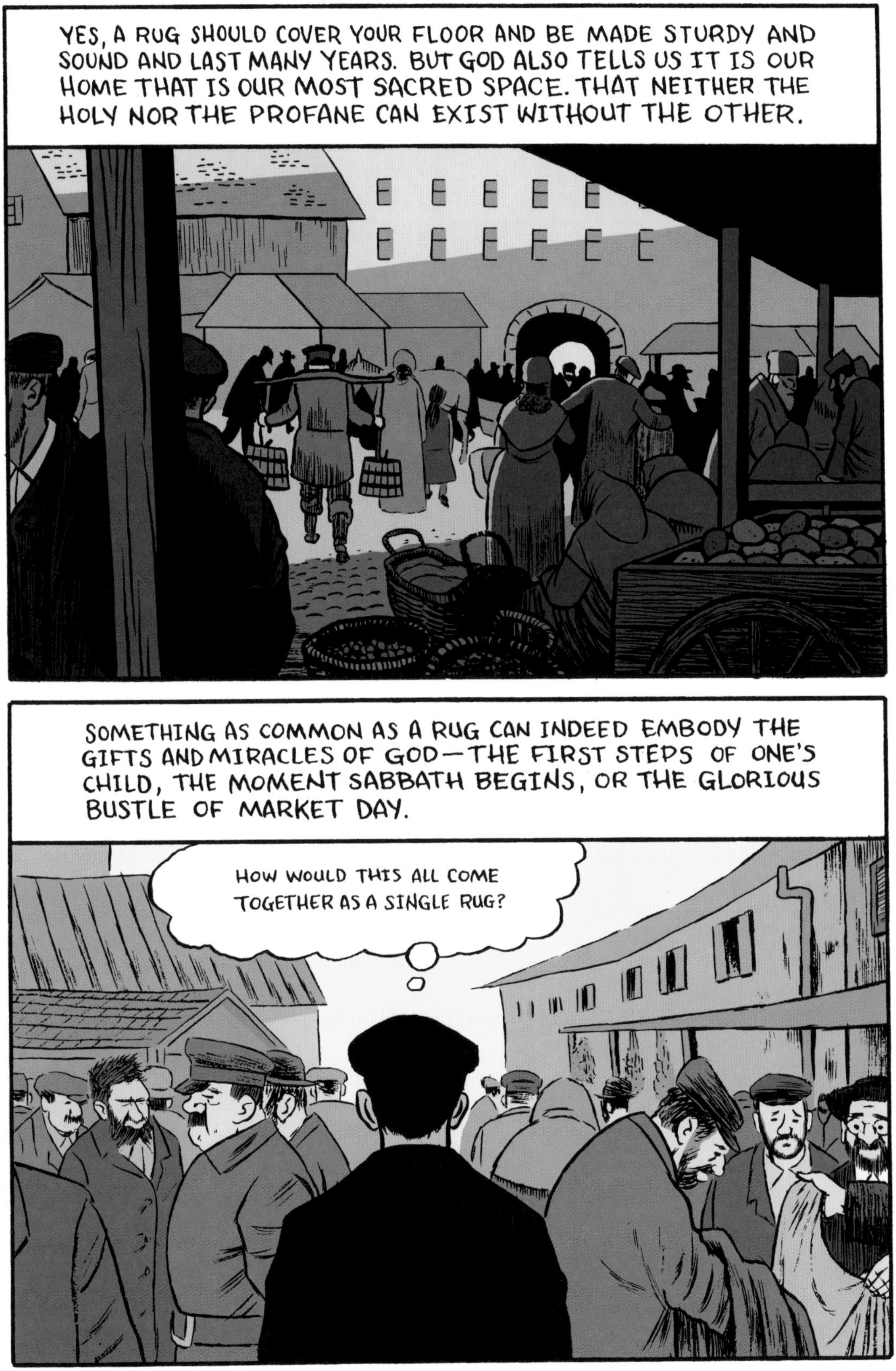
YES, A RUG SHOULD COVER YOUR FLOOR AND BE MADE STURDY AND SOUND AND LAST MANY YEARS. BUT GOD ALSO TELLS US IT IS OUR HOME THAT IS OUR MOST SACRED SPACE. THAT NEITHER THE HOLY NOR THE PROFANE CAN EXIST WITHOUT THE OTHER.
SOMETHING AS COMMON AS A RUG CAN INDEED EMBODY THE GIFTS AND MIRACLES OF GOD—THE FIRST STEPS OF ONE'S CHILD, THE MOMENT SABBATH BEGINS, OR THE GLORIOUS BUSTLE OF MARKET DAY.
HOW WOULD THIS ALL COME TOGETHER AS A SINGLE RUG?

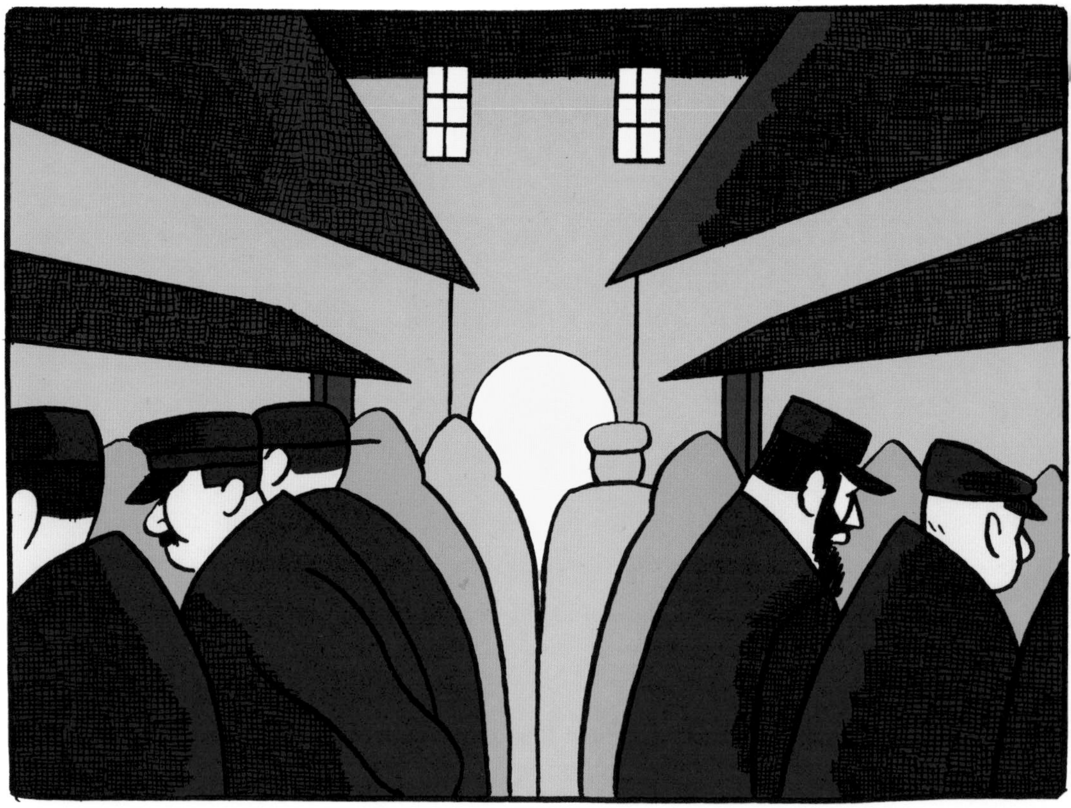

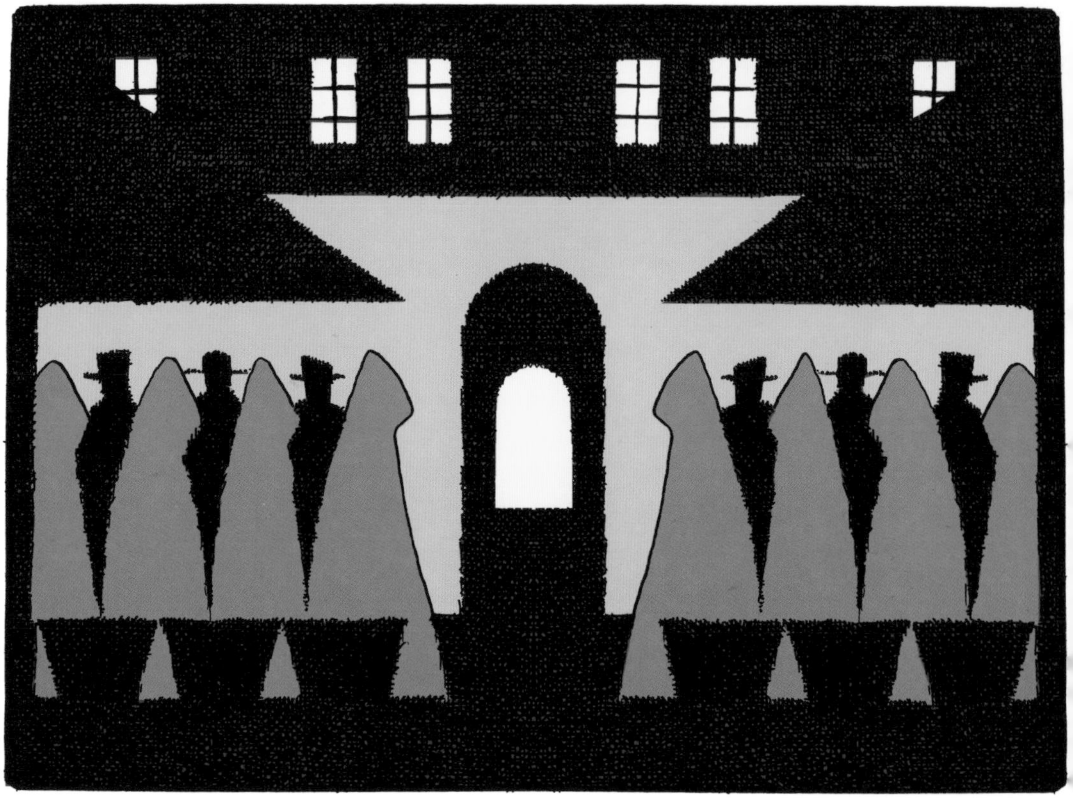

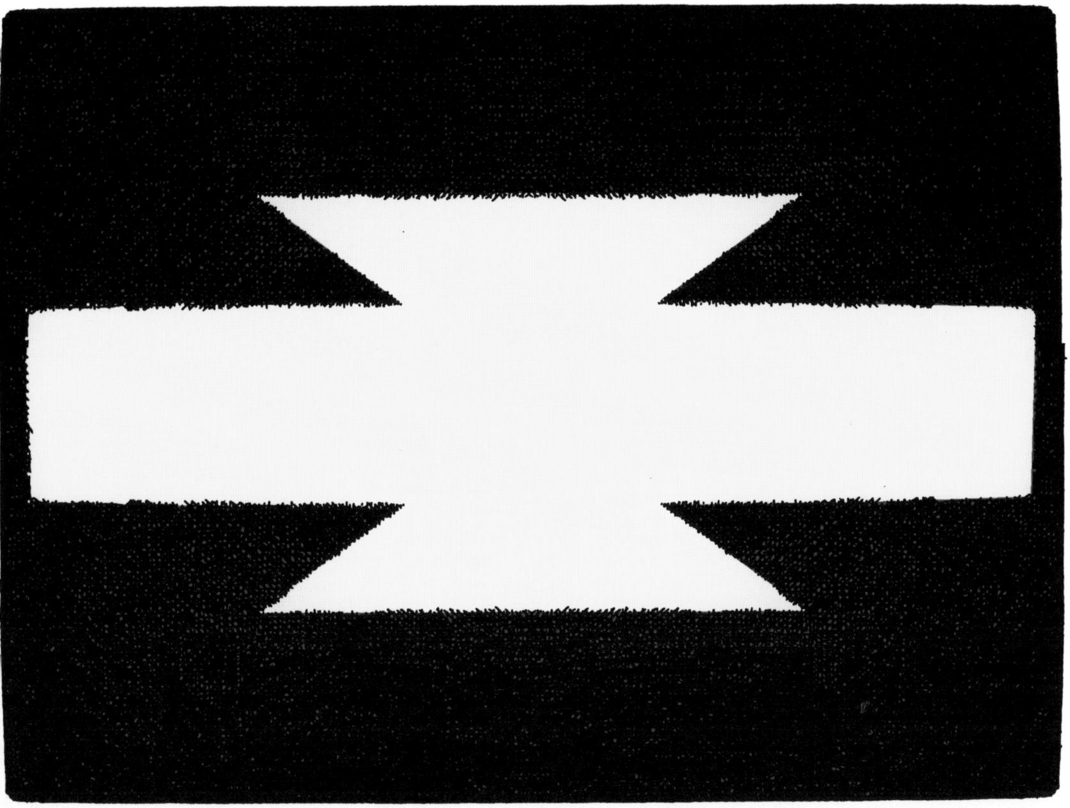

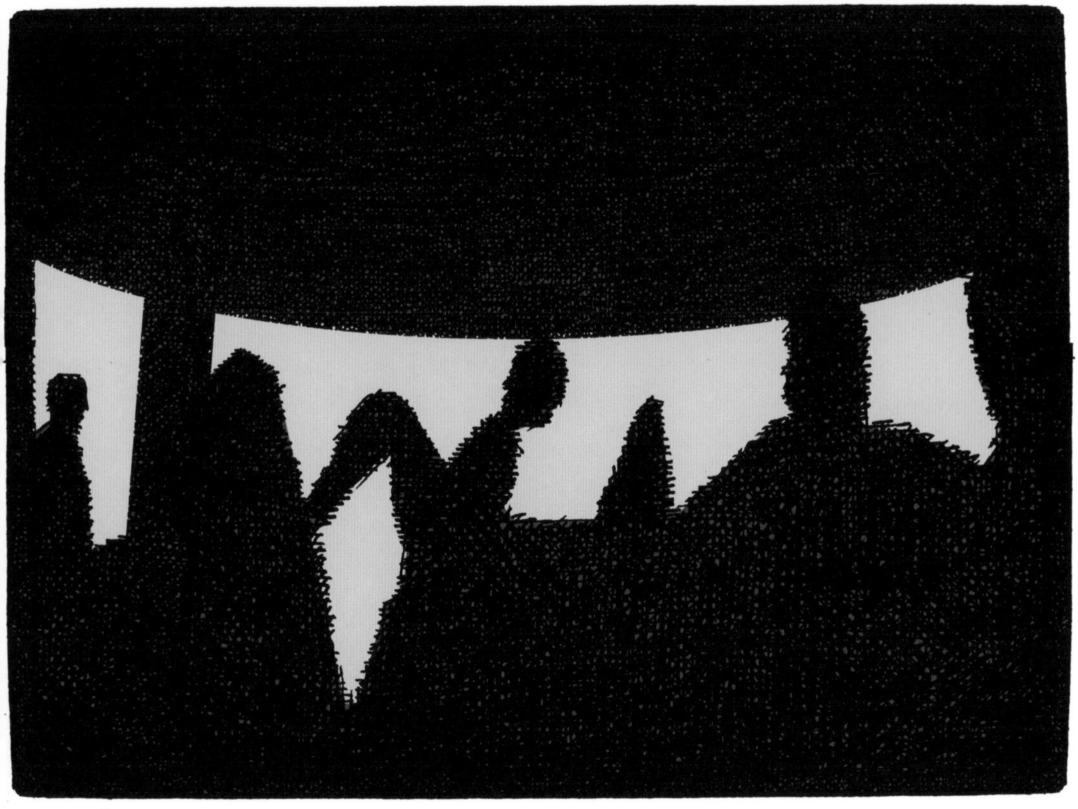

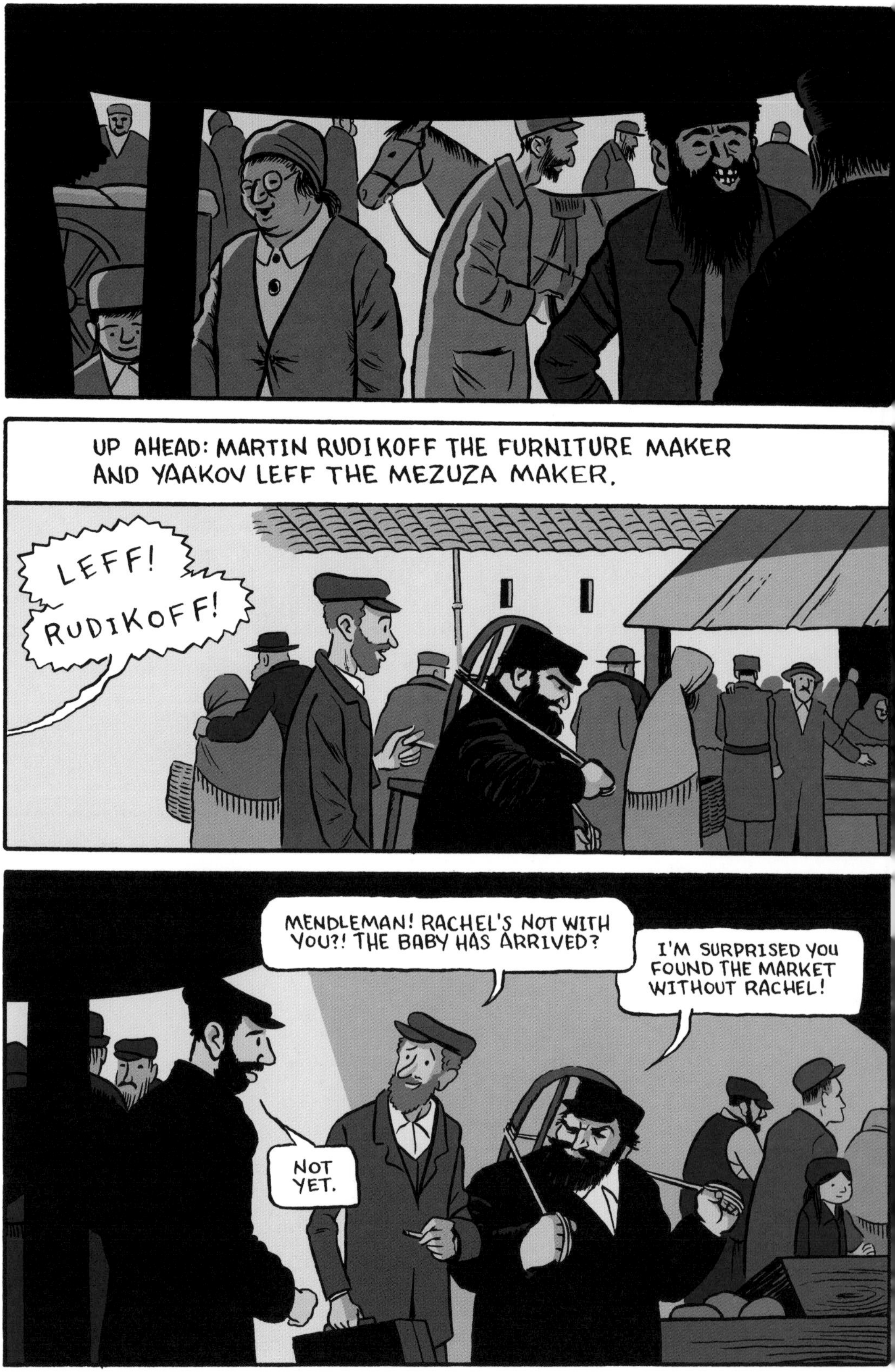
UP AHEAD: MARTIN RUDIKOFF THE FURNITURE MAKER AND YAAKOV LEFF THE MEZUZA MAKER.
LEFF!
RUDIKOFF!
MENDLEMAN! RACHEL'S NOT WITH YOU?! THE BABY HAS ARRIVED?
I'M SURPRISED YOU FOUND THE MARKET WITHOUT RACHEL!
NOT YET.

MY DREAMY NATURE IS A FAVORITE TARGET FOR THEIR SHARP TONGUES. BUT I KNOW BENEATH THEIR TEASING IS A DEEP REGARD—A REGARD THAT IS CERTAINLY MUTUAL. THEY INSPIRE ME TO MAKE EVEN FINER RUGS—TO IMBUE THEM WITH THE SAME BEAUTY AND SPIRIT THAT IS APPARENT IN THEIR WORK.

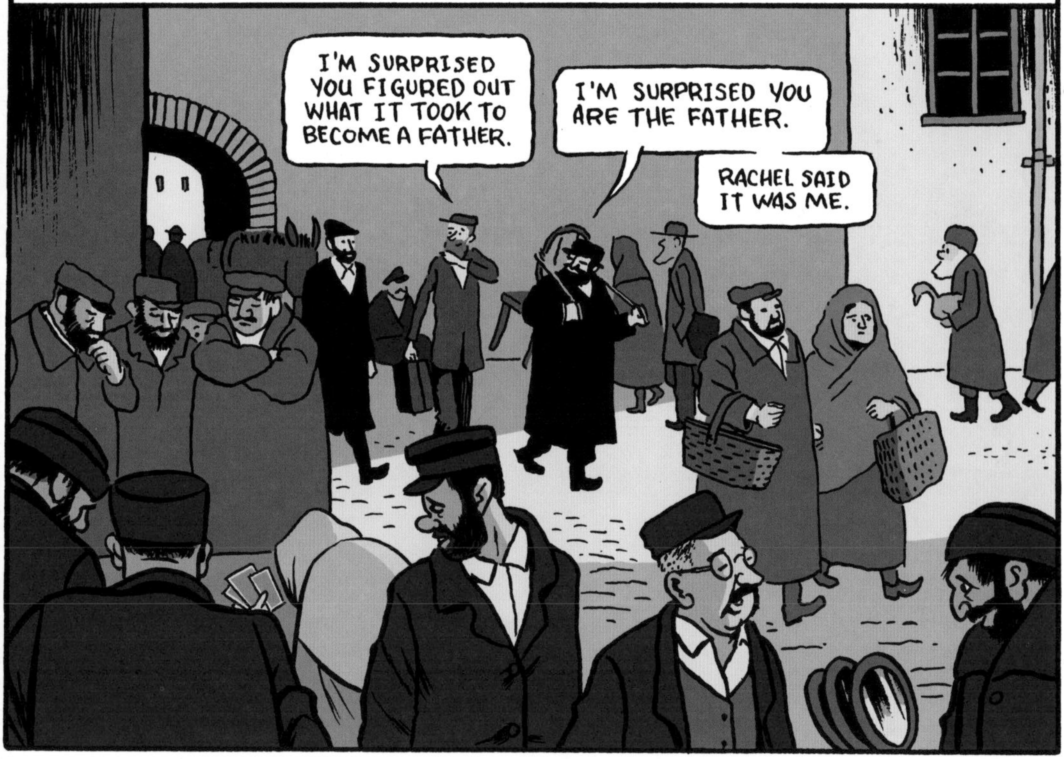
I'M SURPRISED YOU FIGURED OUT WHAT IT TOOK TO BECOME A FATHER.
I'M SURPRISED YOU ARE THE FATHER.
RACHEL SAID IT WAS ME.

WE HAVE ALL COME TO KNOW EACH OTHER THROUGH THE AUSPICES OF ONE ALBERT FINKLER WHOSE SHOP WE NOW HEAD TOWARDS—ALWAYS OUR FIRST STOP ON MARKET DAY.

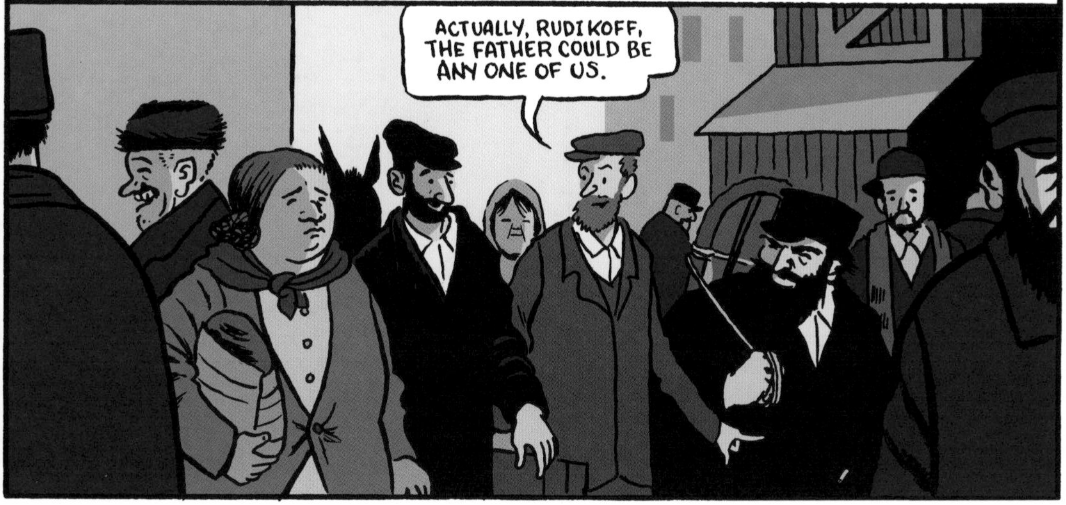
ACTUALLY, RUDIKOFF, THE FATHER COULD BE ANY ONE OF US.

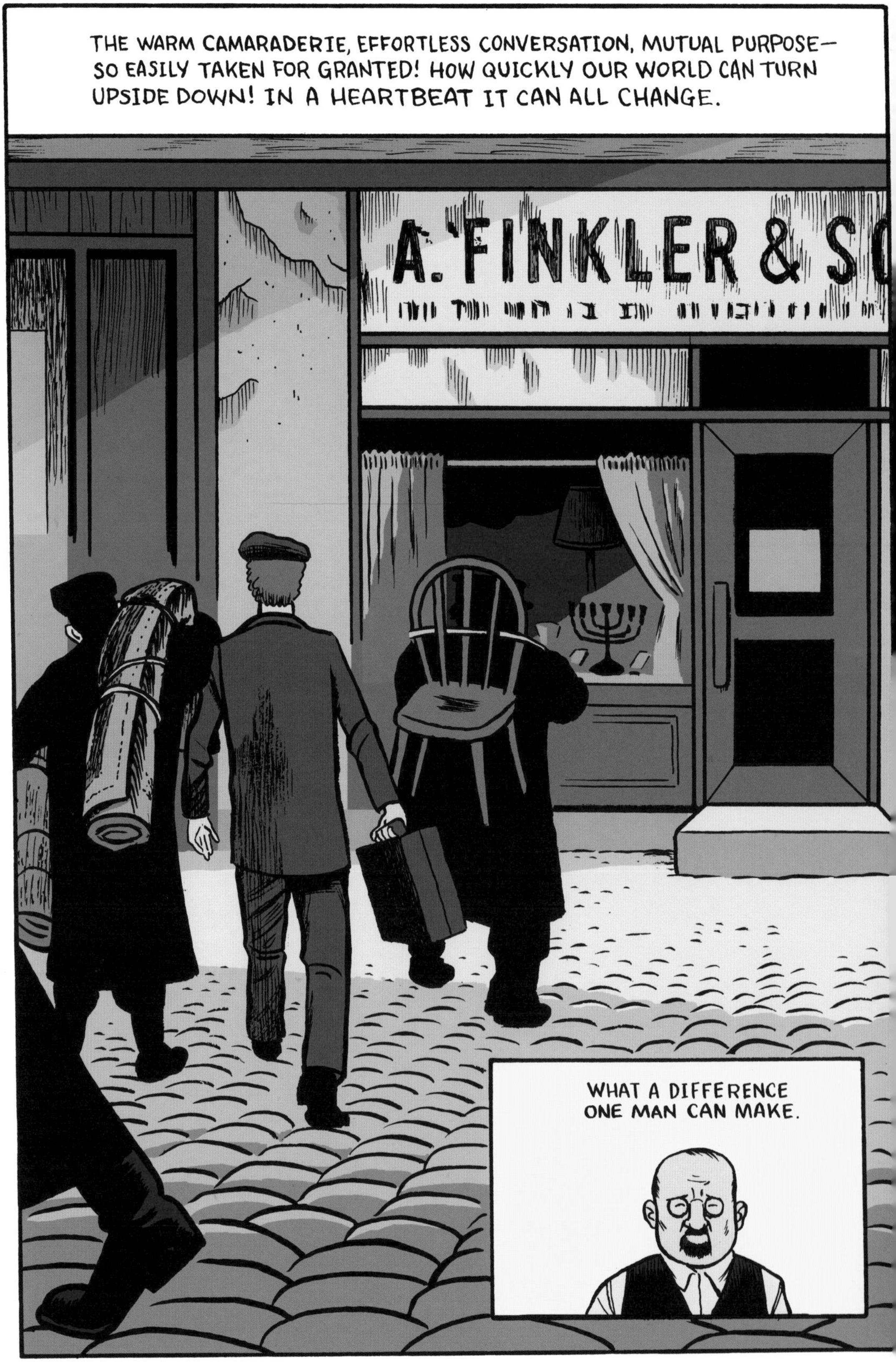
THE WARM CAMARADERIE, EFFORTLESS CONVERSATION, MUTUAL PURPOSE— SO EASILY TAKEN FOR GRANTED! HOW QUICKLY OUR WORLD CAN TURN UPSIDE DOWN! IN A HEARTBEAT IT CAN ALL CHANGE.
A. FINKLER & S
WHAT A DIFFERENCE ONE MAN CAN MAKE.

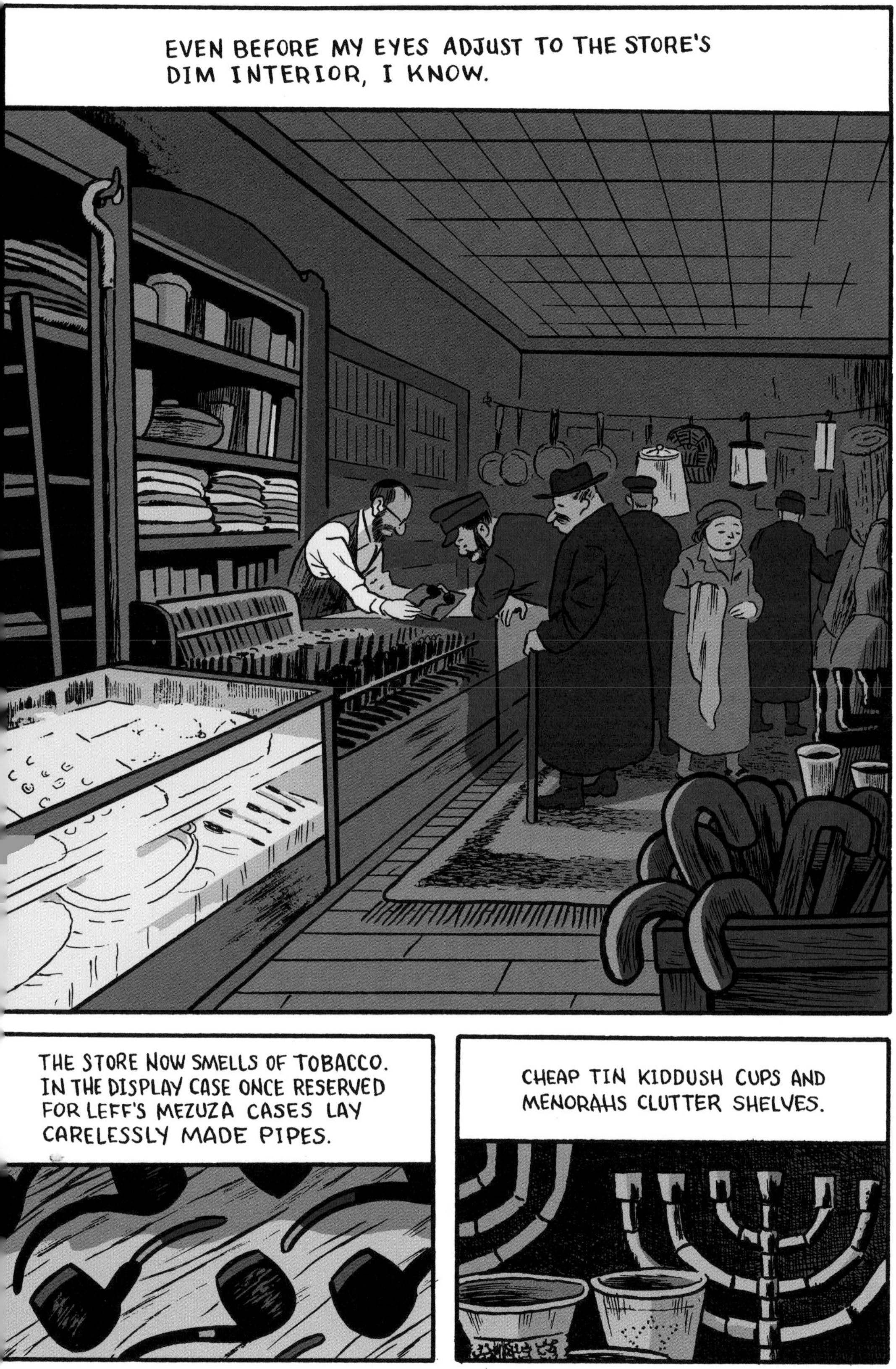
EVEN BEFORE MY EYES ADJUST TO THE STORE'S DIM INTERIOR, I KNOW.
THE STORE NOW SMELLS OF TOBACCO. IN THE DISPLAY CASE ONCE RESERVED FOR LEFF'S MEZUZA CASES LAY CARELESSLY MADE PIPES.
CHEAP TIN KIDDUSH CUPS AND MENORAHS CLUTTER SHELVES.

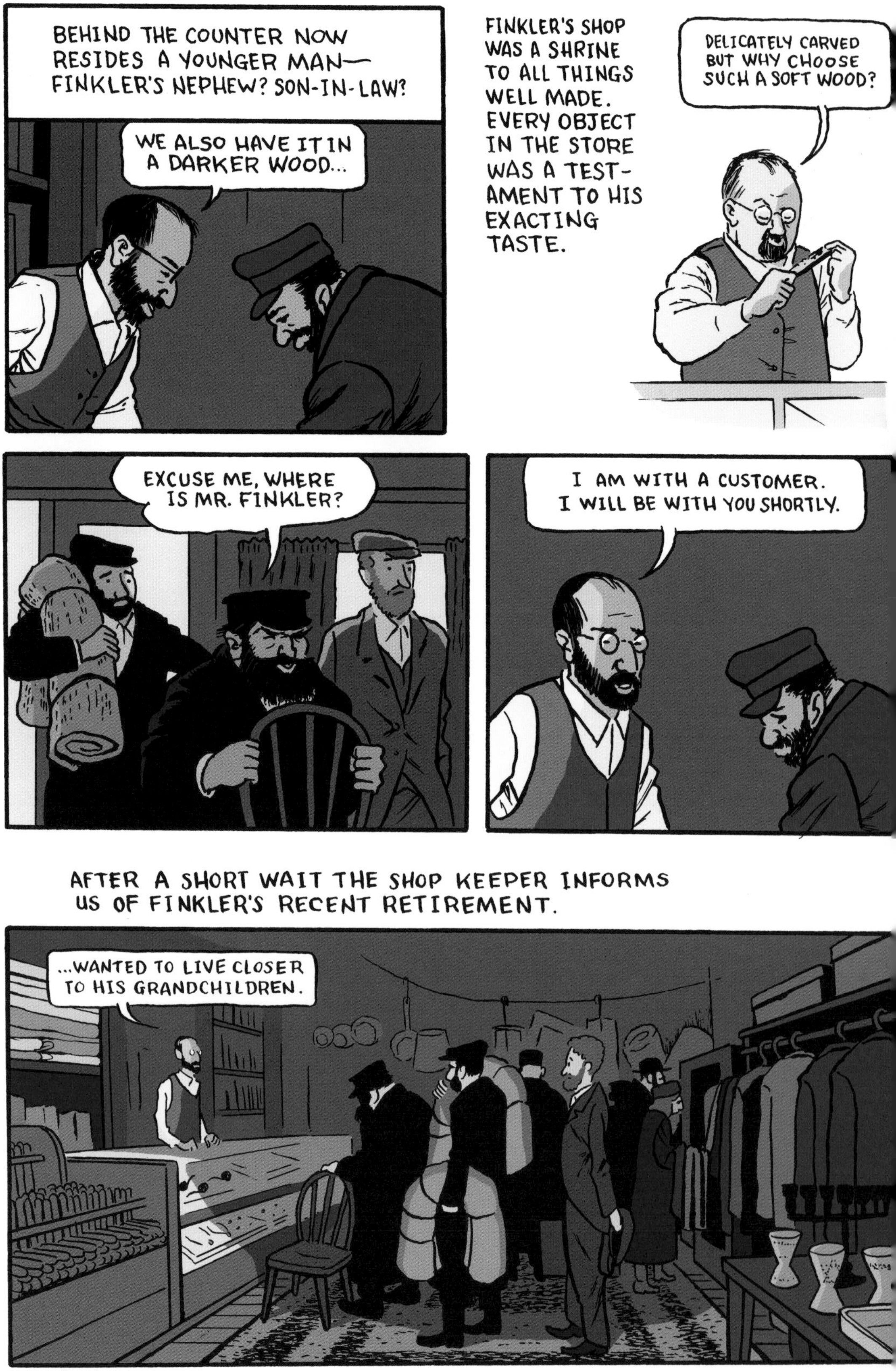
BEHIND THE COUNTER NOW RESIDES A YOUNGER MAN— FINKLER'S NEPHEW? SON-IN-LAW?
WE ALSO HAVE IT IN A DARKER WOOD...
FINKLER'S SHOP WAS A SHRINE TO ALL THINGS WELL MADE. EVERY OBJECT IN THE STORE WAS A TEST-AMENT TO HIS EXACTING TASTE.
DELICATELY CARVED BUT WHY CHOOSE SUCH A SOFT WOOD?
EXCUSE ME, WHERE IS MR. FINKLER?
I AM WITH A CUSTOMER. I WILL BE WITH YOU SHORTLY.
AFTER A SHORT WAIT THE SHOP KEEPER INFORMS US OF FINKLER'S RECENT RETIREMENT.
...WANTED TO LIVE CLOSER TO HIS GRANDCHILDREN.

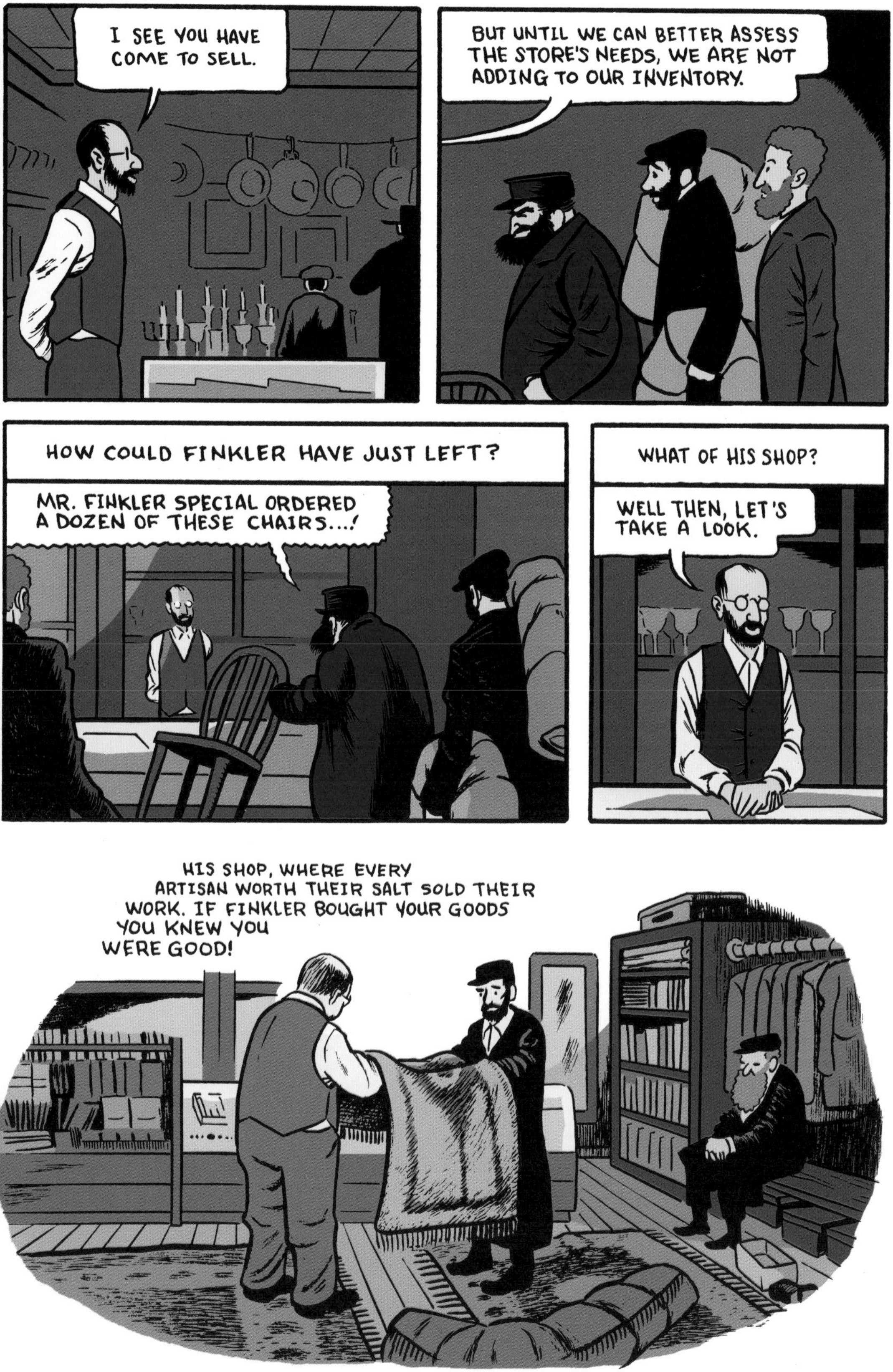
I SEE YOU HAVE COME TO SELL.
BUT UNTIL WE CAN BETTER ASSESS THE STORE'S NEEDS, WE ARE NOT ADDING TO OUR INVENTORY.
HOW COULD FINKLER HAVE JUST LEFT?
MR. FINKLER SPECIAL ORDERED A DOZEN OF THESE CHAIRS...!
WHAT OF HIS SHOP?
WELL THEN, LET'S TAKE A LOOK.
HIS SHOP, WHERE EVERY ARTISAN WORTH THEIR SALT SOLD THEIR WORK. IF FINKLER BOUGHT YOUR GOODS YOU KNEW YOU WERE GOOD!

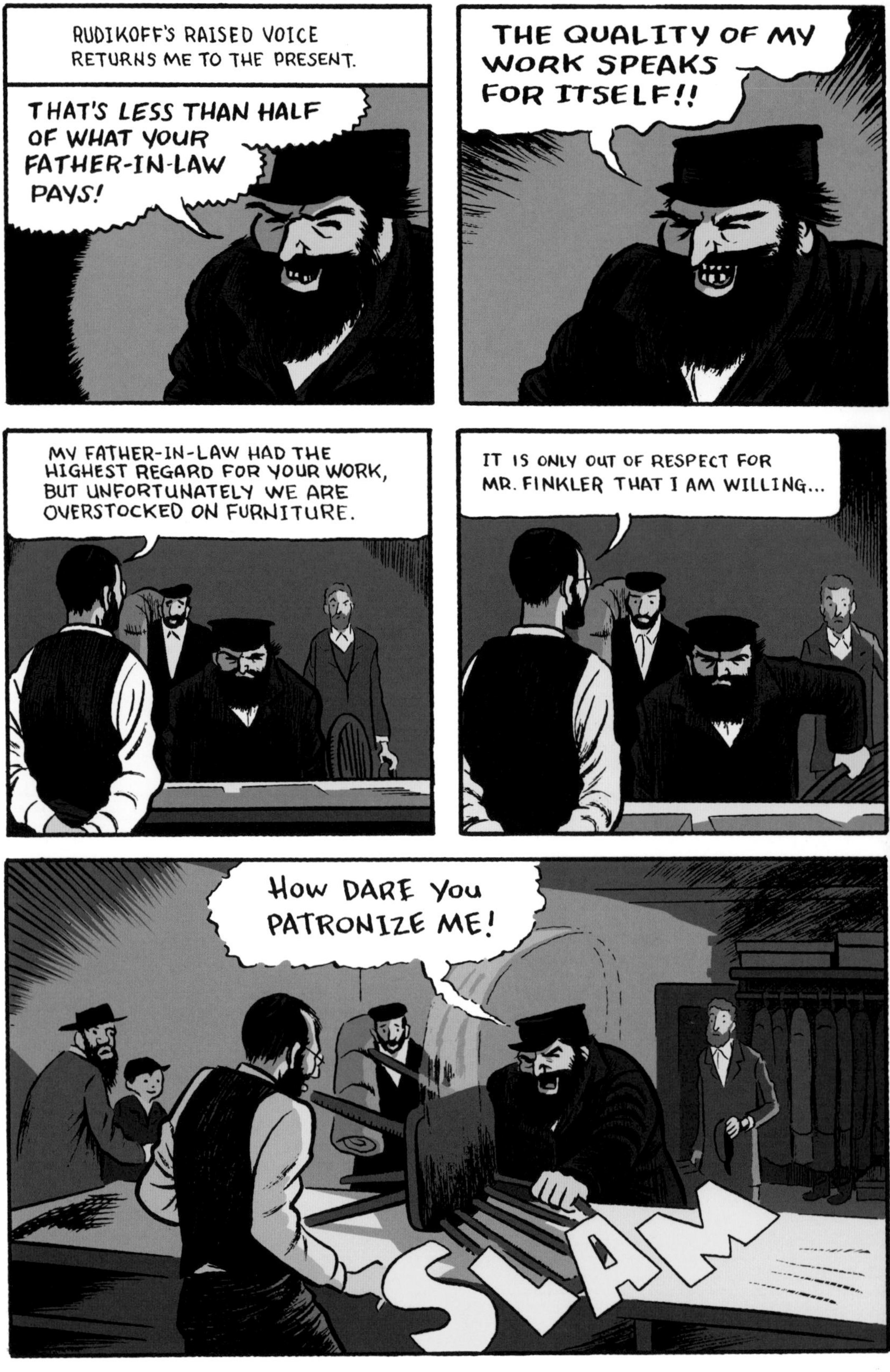
RUDIKOFF'S RAISED VOICE RETURNS ME TO THE PRESENT.
THAT'S LESS THAN HALF OF WHAT YOUR FATHER-IN-LAW PAYS!
THE QUALITY OF MY WORK SPEAKS FOR ITSELF!!
MY FATHER-IN-LAW HAD THE HIGHEST REGARD FOR YOUR WORK, BUT UNFORTUNATELY WE ARE OVERSTOCKED ON FURNITURE.
IT IS ONLY OUT OF RESPECT FOR MR. FINKLER THAT I AM WILLING...
HOW DARE YOU PATRONIZE ME!
SLAM

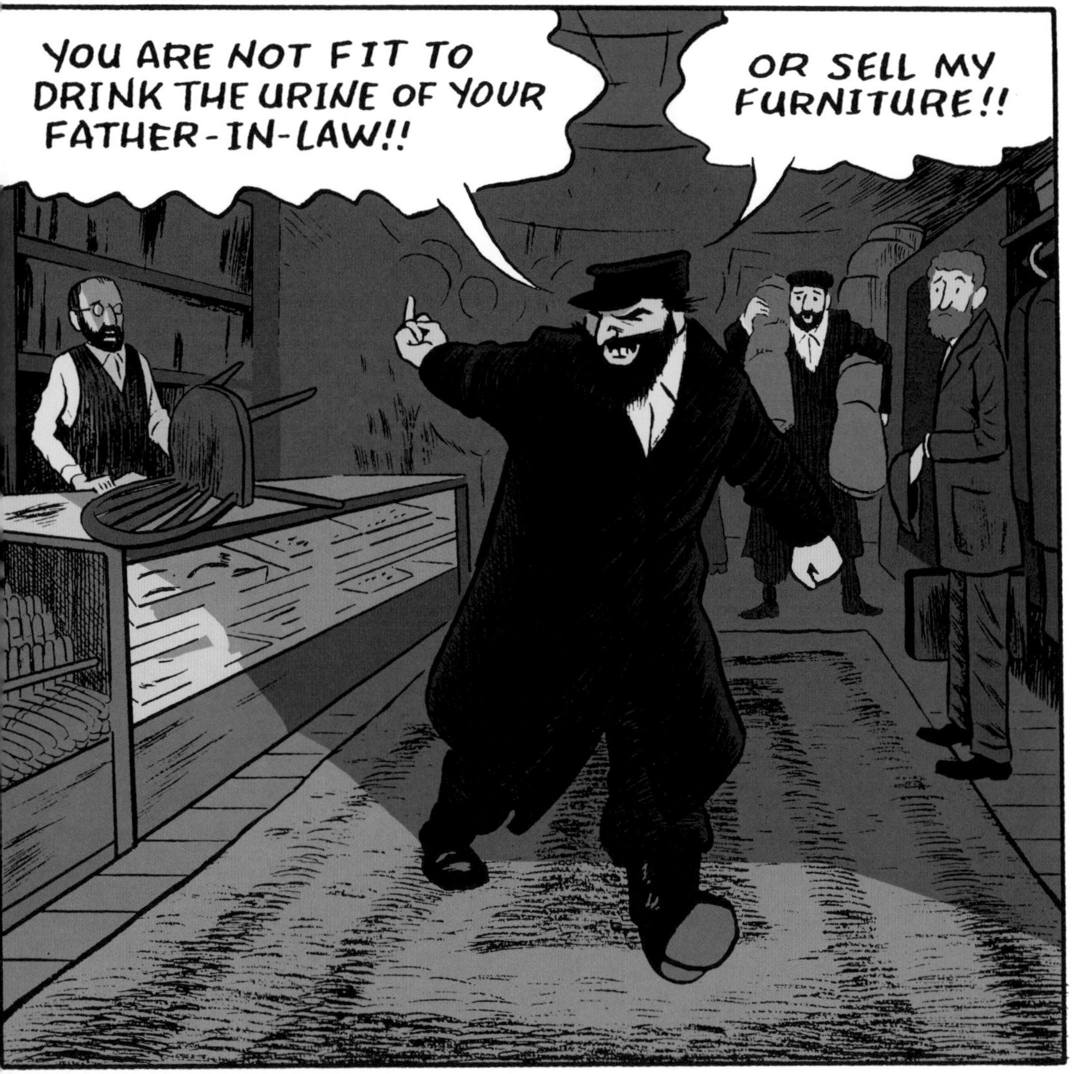
YOU ARE NOT FIT TO DRINK THE URINE OF YOUR FATHER-IN-LAW!!
OR SELL MY FURNITURE!!

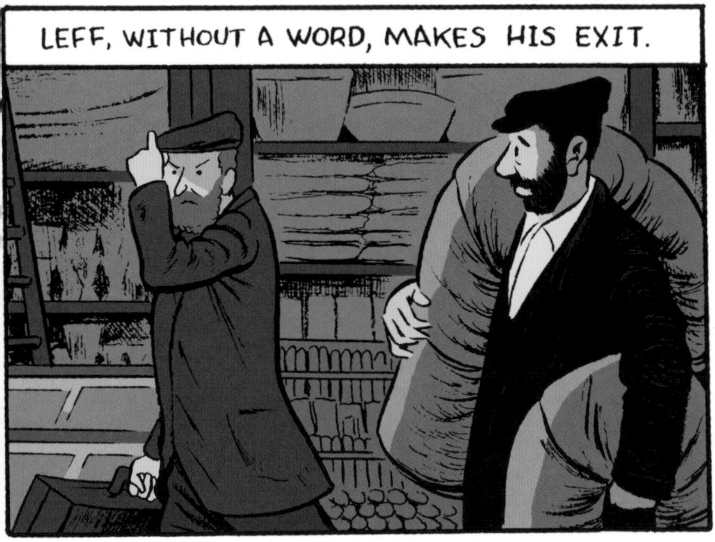
LEFF, WITHOUT A WORD, MAKES HIS EXIT.

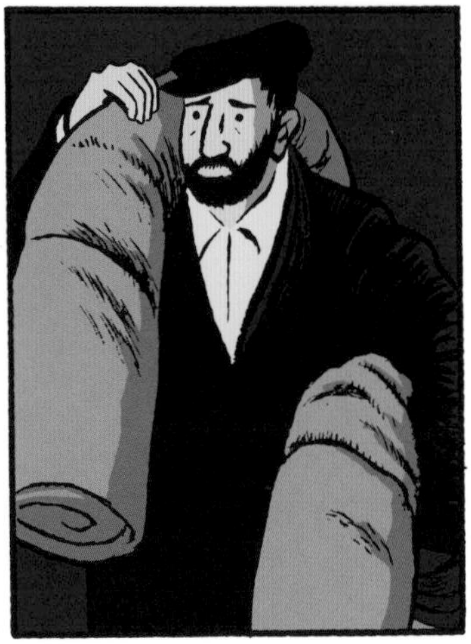
I WANT TO FOLLOW.

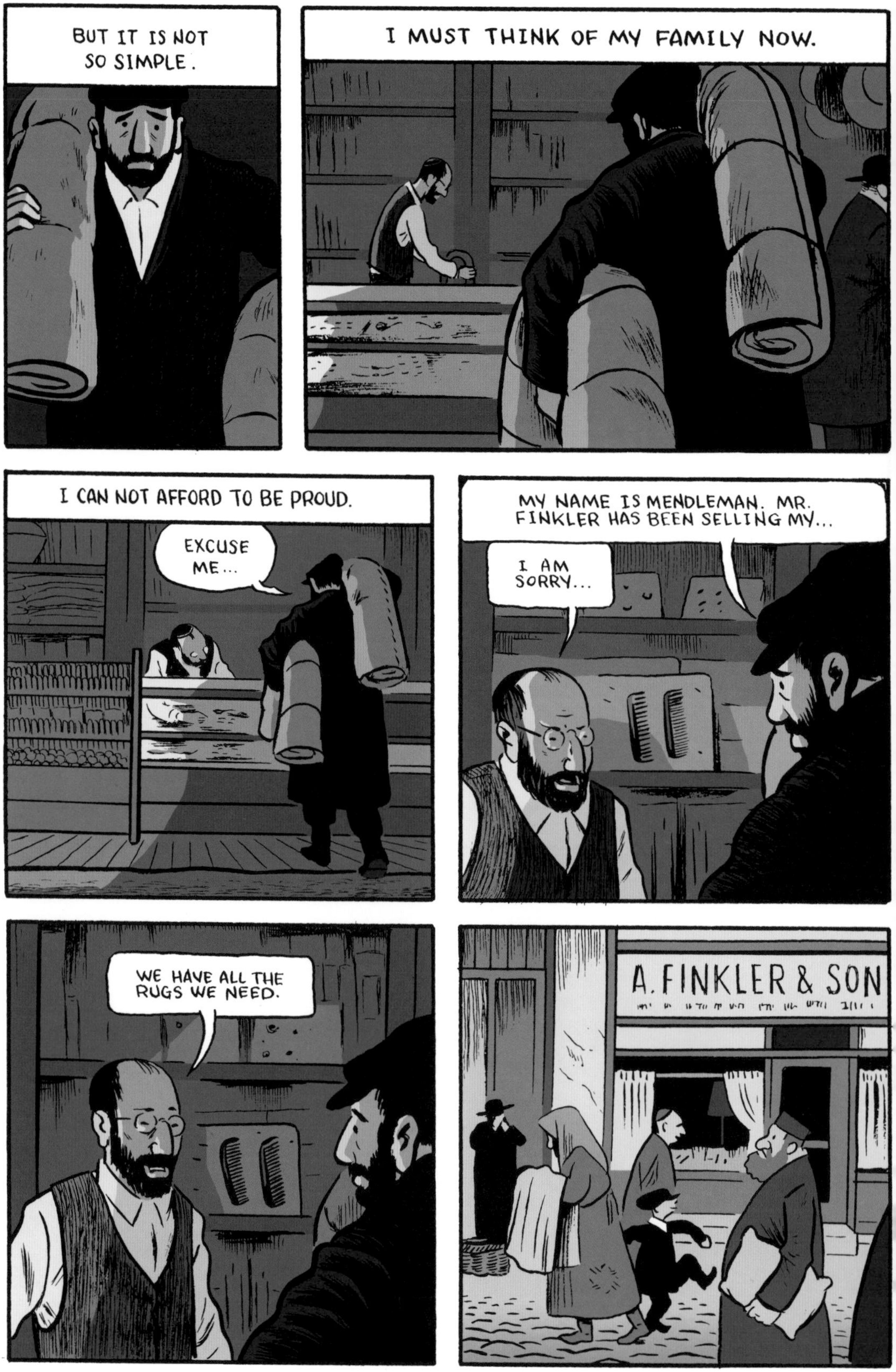
BUT IT IS NOT SO SIMPLE.
I MUST THINK OF MY FAMILY NOW.
I CAN NOT AFFORD TO BE PROUD.
EXCUSE ME...
MY NAME IS MENDLEMAN. MR. FINKLER HAS BEEN SELLING MY...
I AM SORRY...
WE HAVE ALL THE RUGS WE NEED.
A. FINKLER & SON

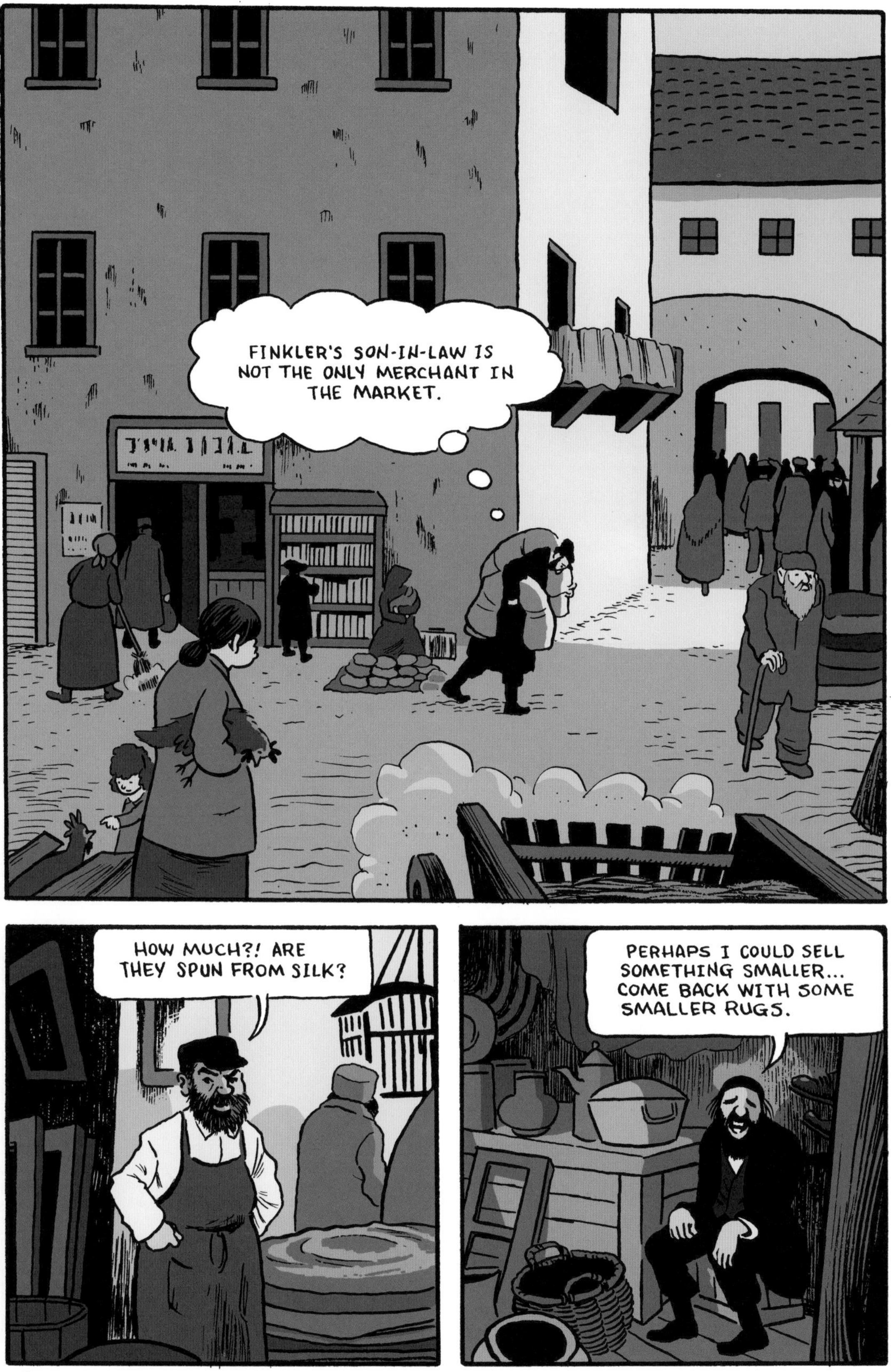
FINKLER'S SON-IN-LAW IS NOT THE ONLY MERCHANT IN THE MARKET.
HOW MUCH?! ARE THEY SPUN FROM SILK?
PERHAPS I COULD SELL SOMETHING SMALLER... COME BACK WITH SOME SMALLER RUGS.

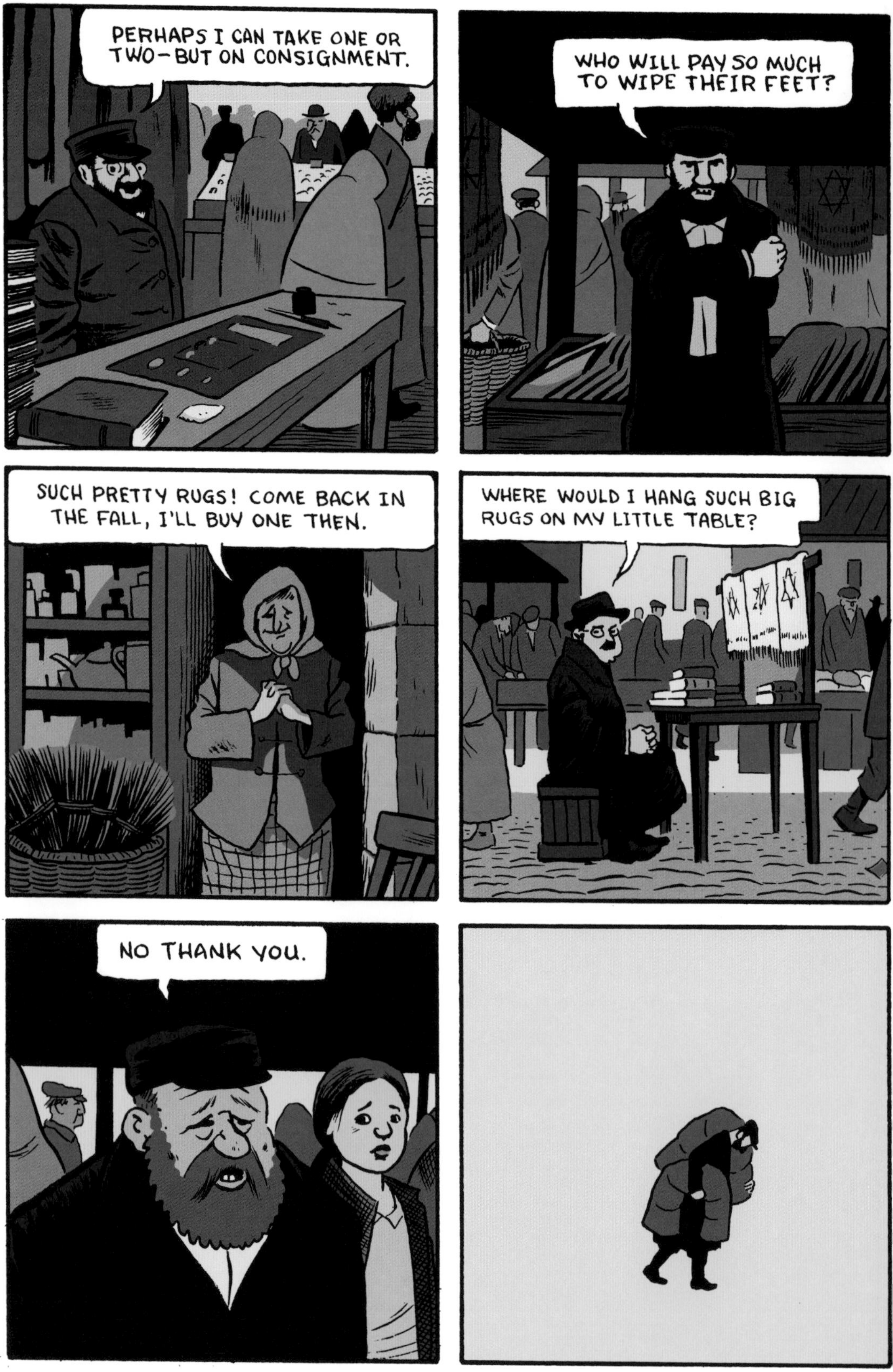
PERHAPS I CAN TAKE ONE OR TWO—BUT ON CONSIGNMENT.
WHO WILL PAY SO MUCH TO WIPE THEIR FEET?
SUCH PRETTY RUGS! COME BACK IN THE FALL, I'LL BUY ONE THEN.
WHERE WOULD I HANG SUCH BIG RUGS ON MY LITTLE TABLE?
NO THANK YOU.

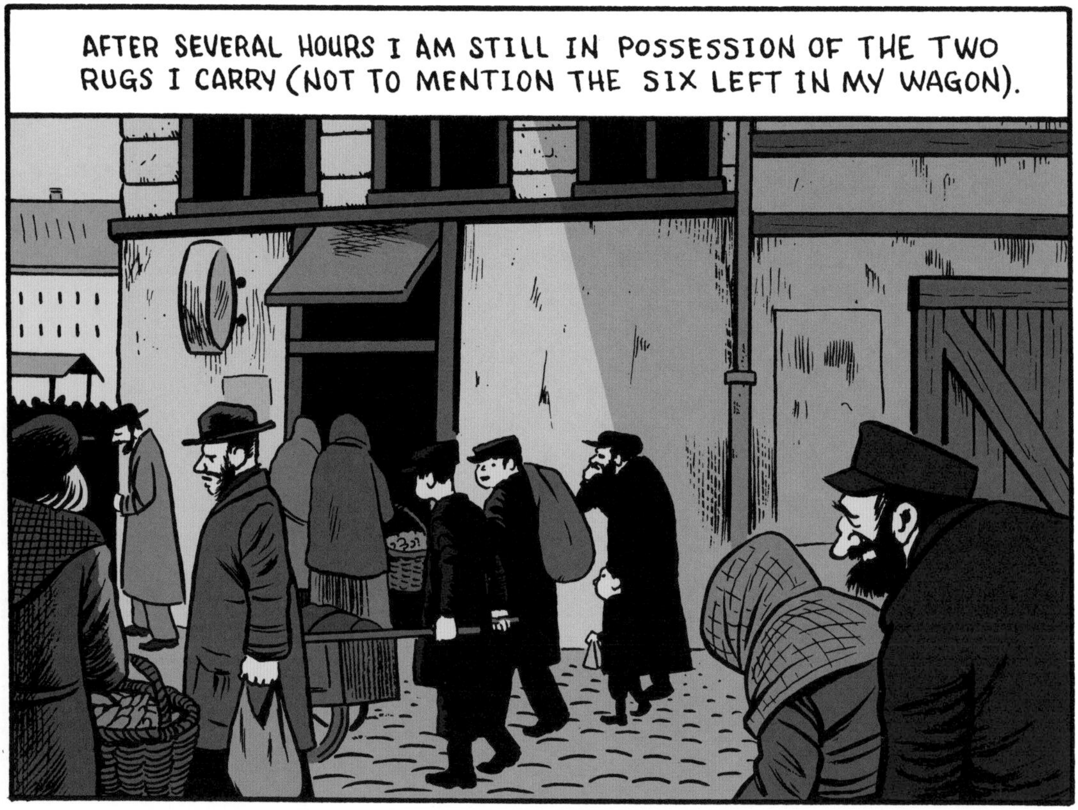
AFTER SEVERAL HOURS I AM STILL IN POSSESSION OF THE TWO RUGS I CARRY (NOT TO MENTION THE SIX LEFT IN MY WAGON).

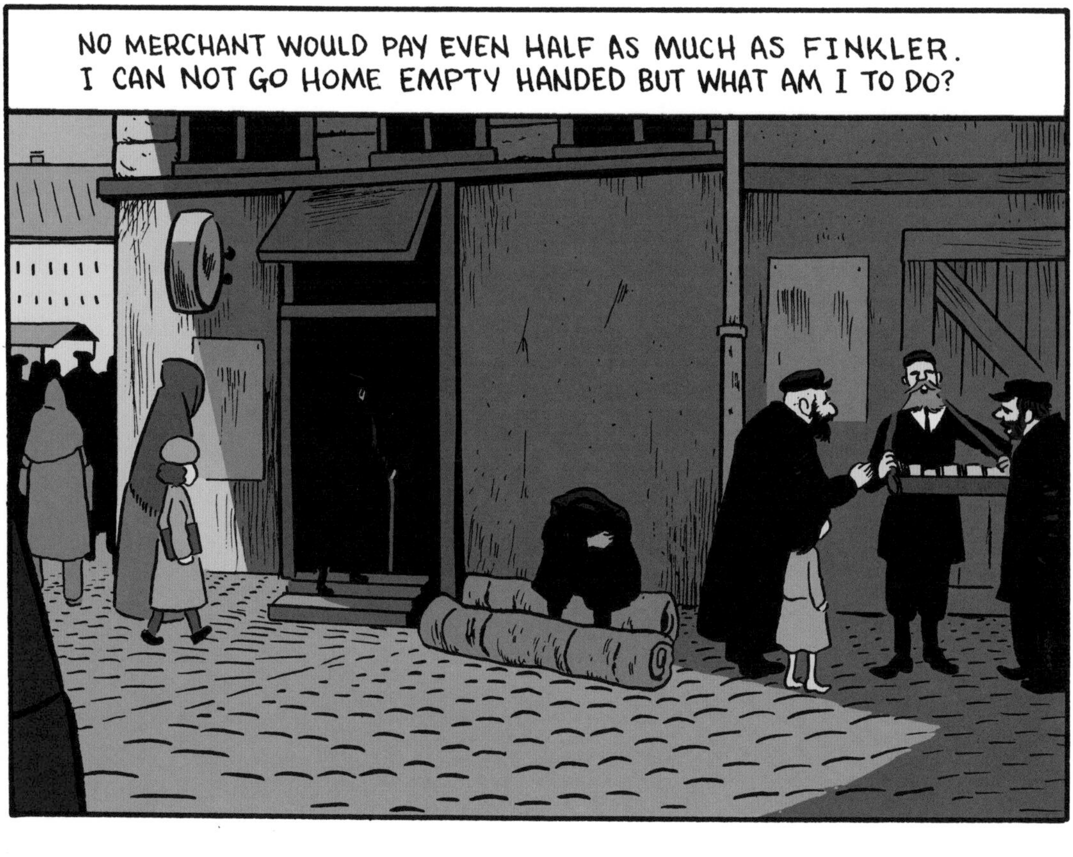
NO MERCHANT WOULD PAY EVEN HALF AS MUCH AS FINKLER. I CAN NOT GO HOME EMPTY HANDED BUT WHAT AM I TO DO?

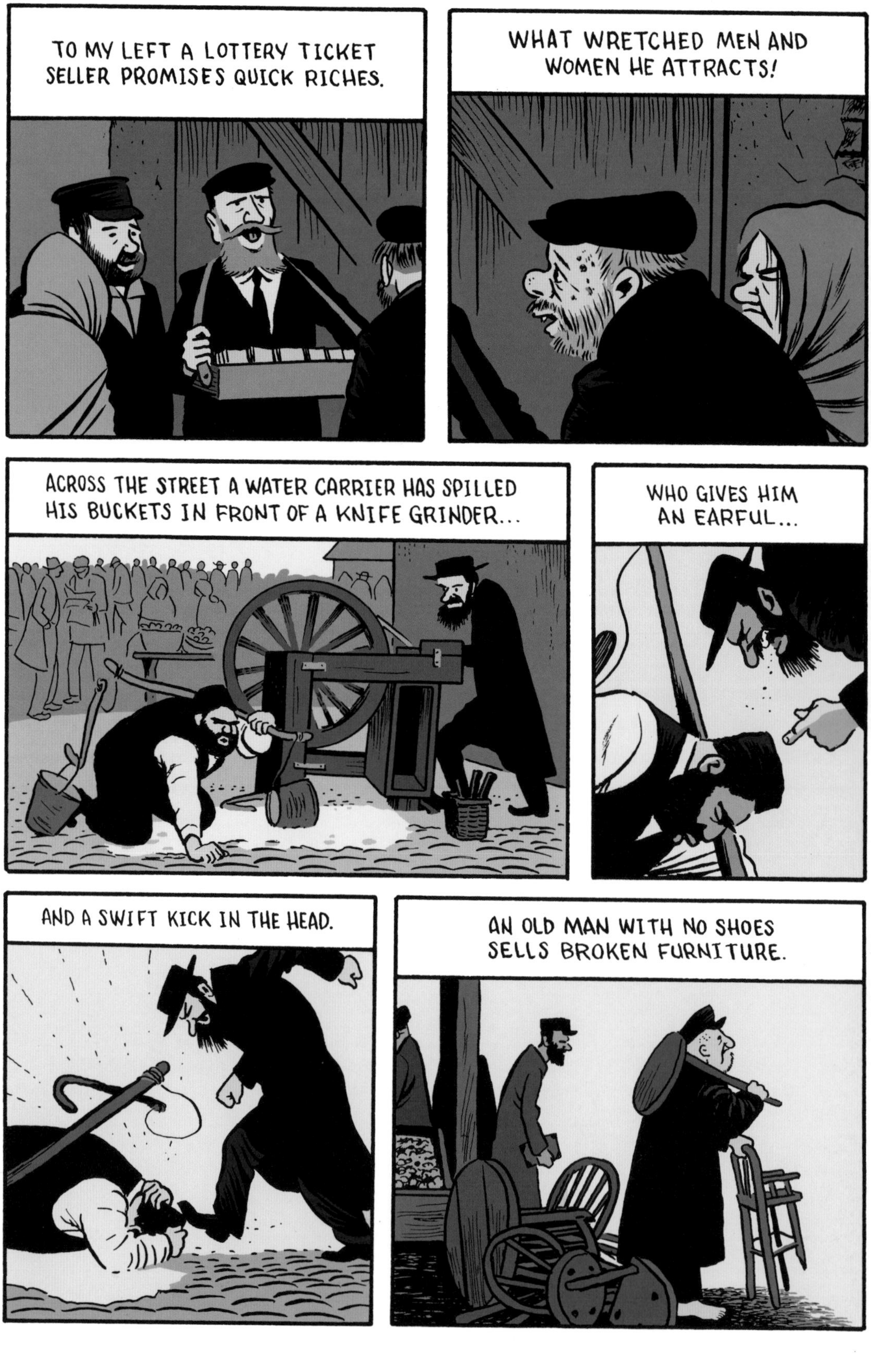
TO MY LEFT A LOTTERY TICKET SELLER PROMISES QUICK RICHES.
WHAT WRETCHED MEN AND WOMEN HE ATTRACTS!
ACROSS THE STREET A WATER CARRIER HAS SPILLED HIS BUCKETS IN FRONT OF A KNIFE GRINDER...
WHO GIVES HIM AN EARFUL...
AND A SWIFT KICK IN THE HEAD.
AN OLD MAN WITH NO SHOES SELLS BROKEN FURNITURE.

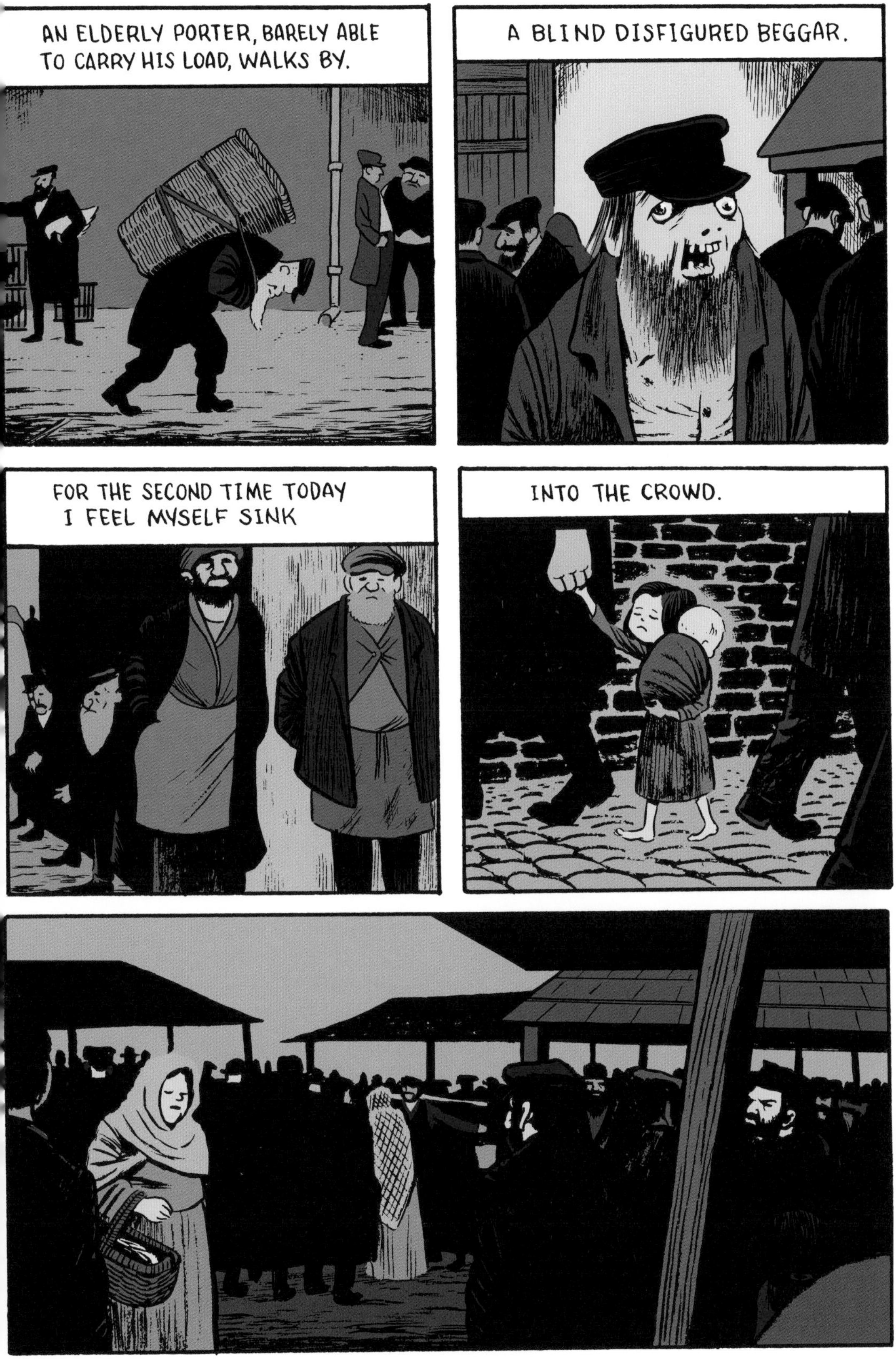
AN ELDERLY PORTER, BARELY ABLE TO CARRY HIS LOAD, WALKS BY.
A BLIND DISFIGURED BEGGAR.
FOR THE SECOND TIME TODAY I FEEL MYSELF SINK
INTO THE CROWD.

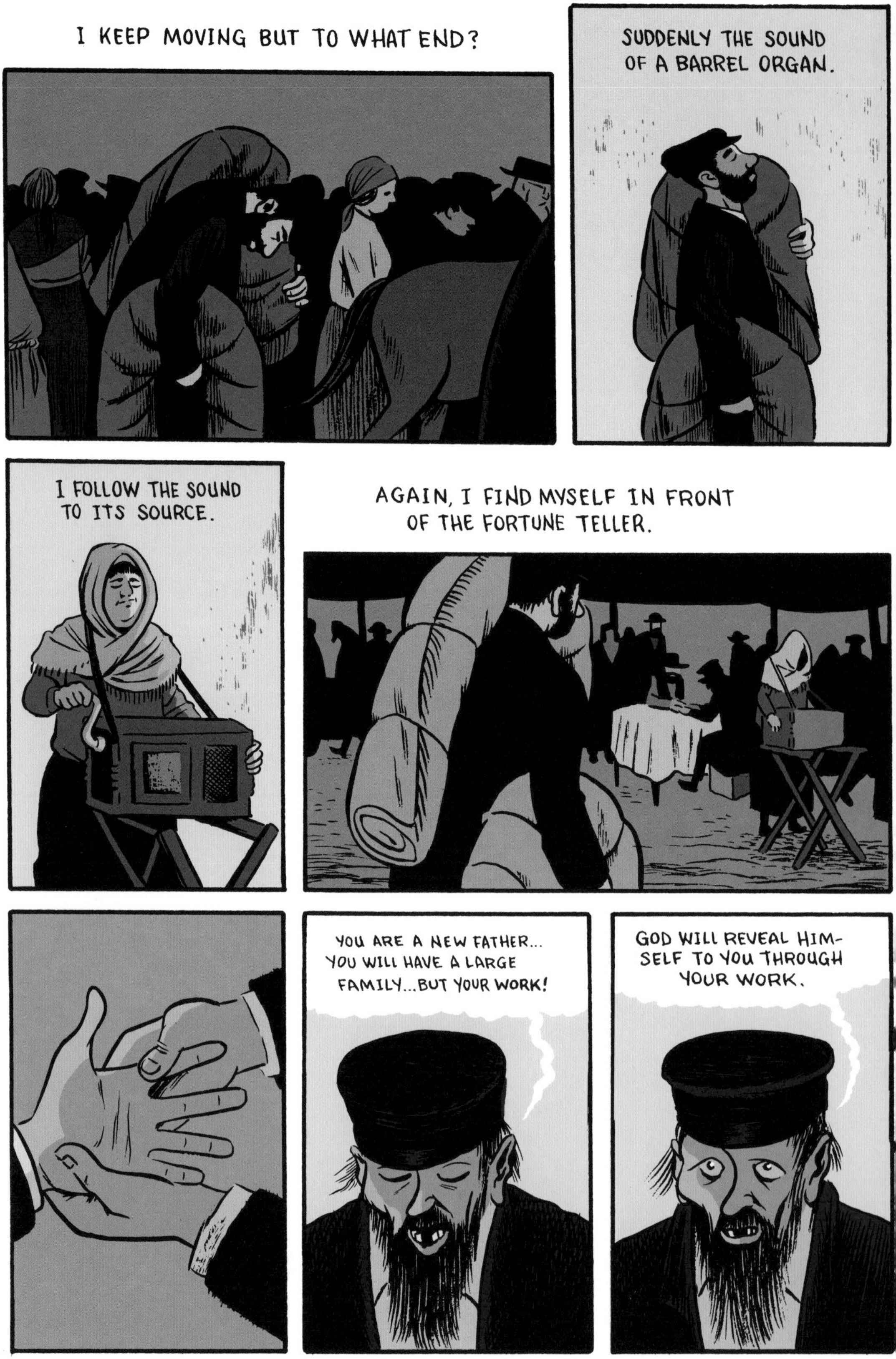
I KEEP MOVING BUT TO WHAT END?
SUDDENLY THE SOUND OF A BARREL ORGAN.
I FOLLOW THE SOUND TO ITS SOURCE.
AGAIN, I FIND MYSELF IN FRONT OF THE FORTUNE TELLER.
YOU ARE A NEW FATHER... YOU WILL HAVE A LARGE FAMILY...BUT YOUR WORK!
GOD WILL REVEAL HIM-SELF TO YOU THROUGH YOUR WORK.

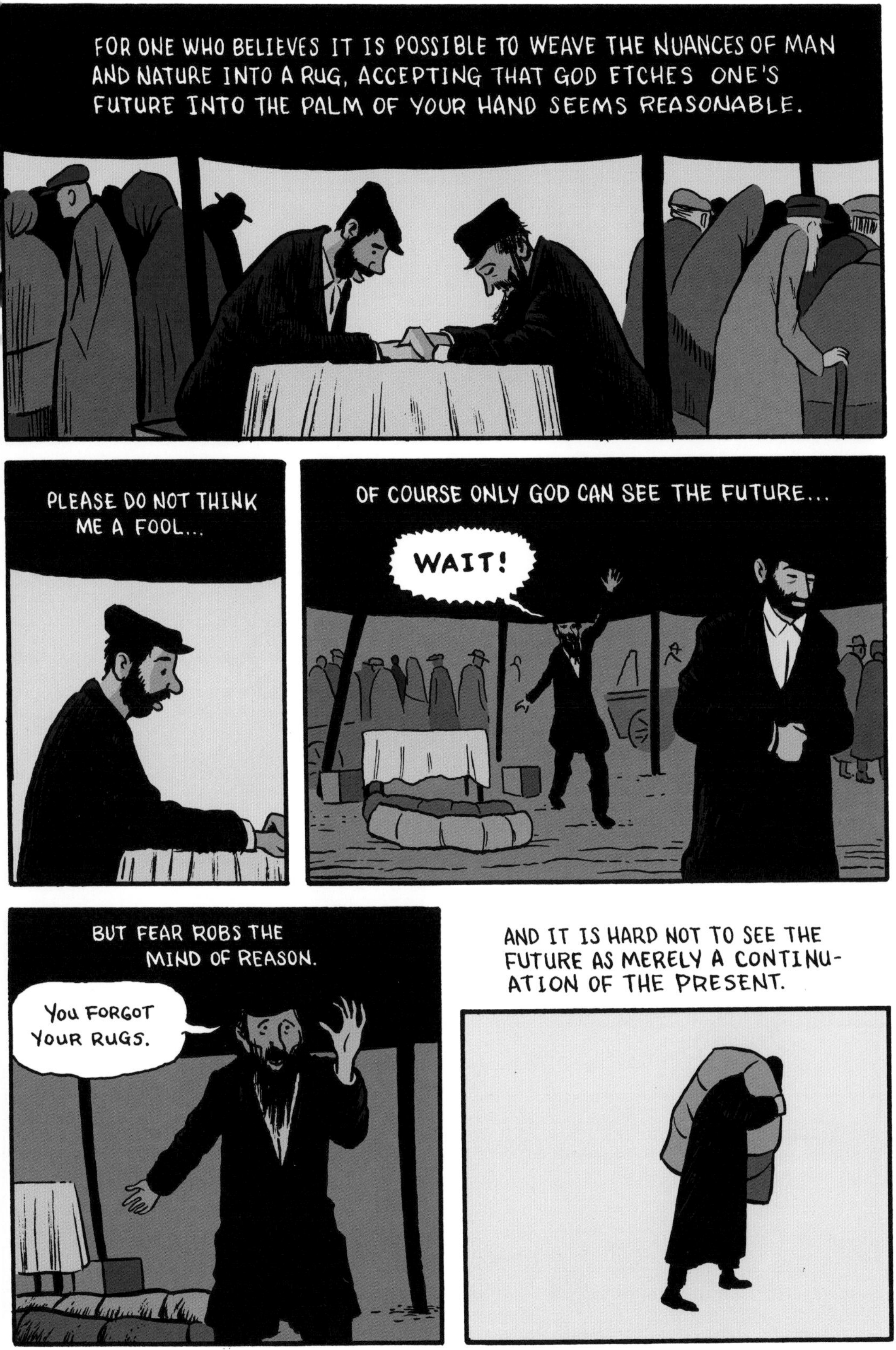
FOR ONE WHO BELIEVES IT IS POSSIBLE TO WEAVE THE NUANCES OF MAN AND NATURE INTO A RUG, ACCEPTING THAT GOD ETCHES ONE'S FUTURE INTO THE PALM OF YOUR HAND SEEMS REASONABLE.
PLEASE DO NOT THINK ME A FOOL...
OF COURSE ONLY GOD CAN SEE THE FUTURE...
WAIT!
BUT FEAR ROBS THE MIND OF REASON.
YOU FORGOT YOUR RUGS.
AND IT IS HARD NOT TO SEE THE FUTURE AS MERELY A CONTINUATION OF THE PRESENT.

THE PRESENT.	THE MISERABLE PRESENT.

THE STENCH.	THE SUFFERING.	MY UNCOMFOR-TABLY FULL BLADDER.

  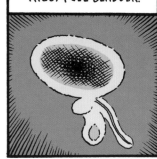

MY HEEL, CHAFING AGAINST THE BACK OF MY BOOT.	A MELANCHOLY FOOL.	A MAN HAWKING CHILDREN'S TOYS

WHICH I CAN NO LONGER AFFORD	HAVING SPENT MY LAST FEW COINS	ON A FORTUNE TELLER.

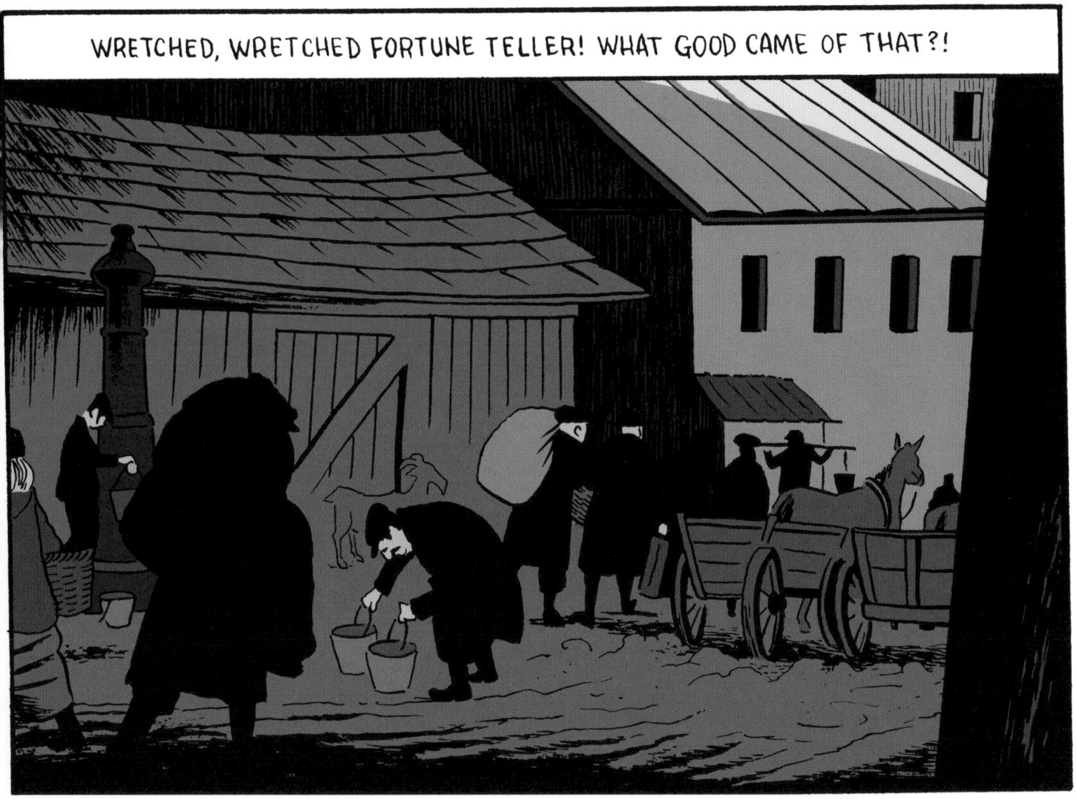
WRETCHED, WRETCHED FORTUNE TELLER! WHAT GOOD CAME OF THAT?!

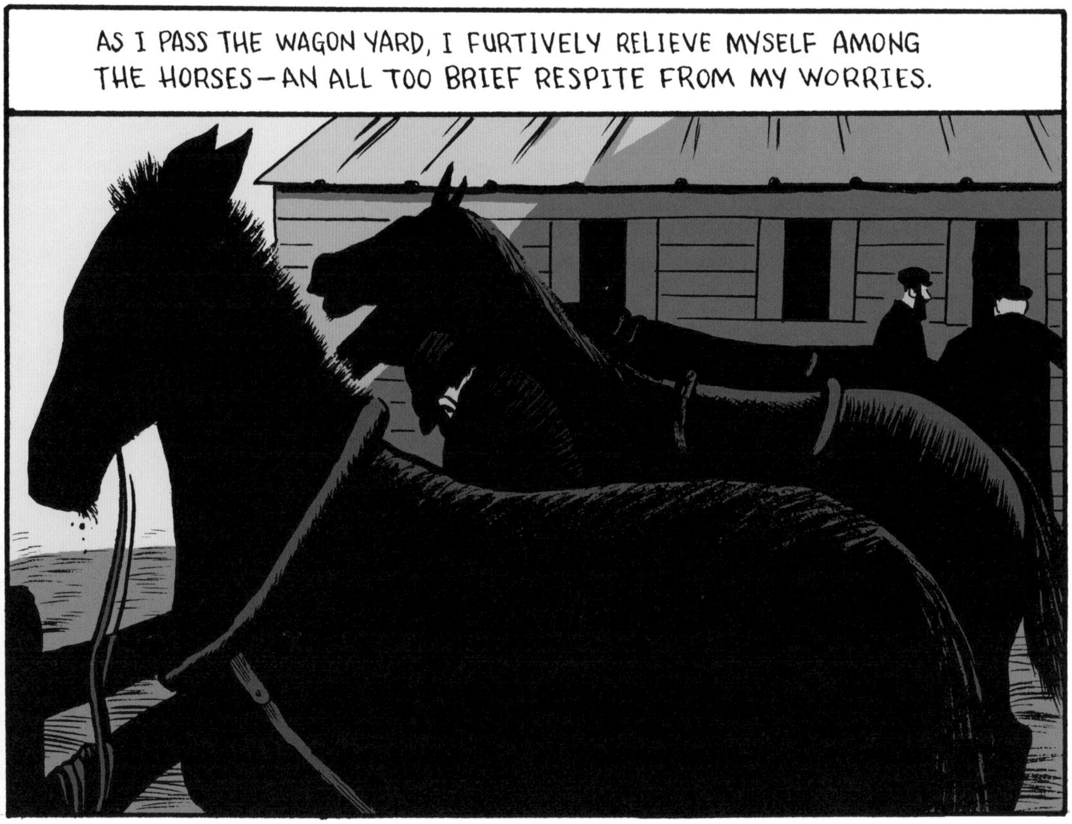
AS I PASS THE WAGON YARD, I FURTIVELY RELIEVE MYSELF AMONG THE HORSES—AN ALL TOO BRIEF RESPITE FROM MY WORRIES.

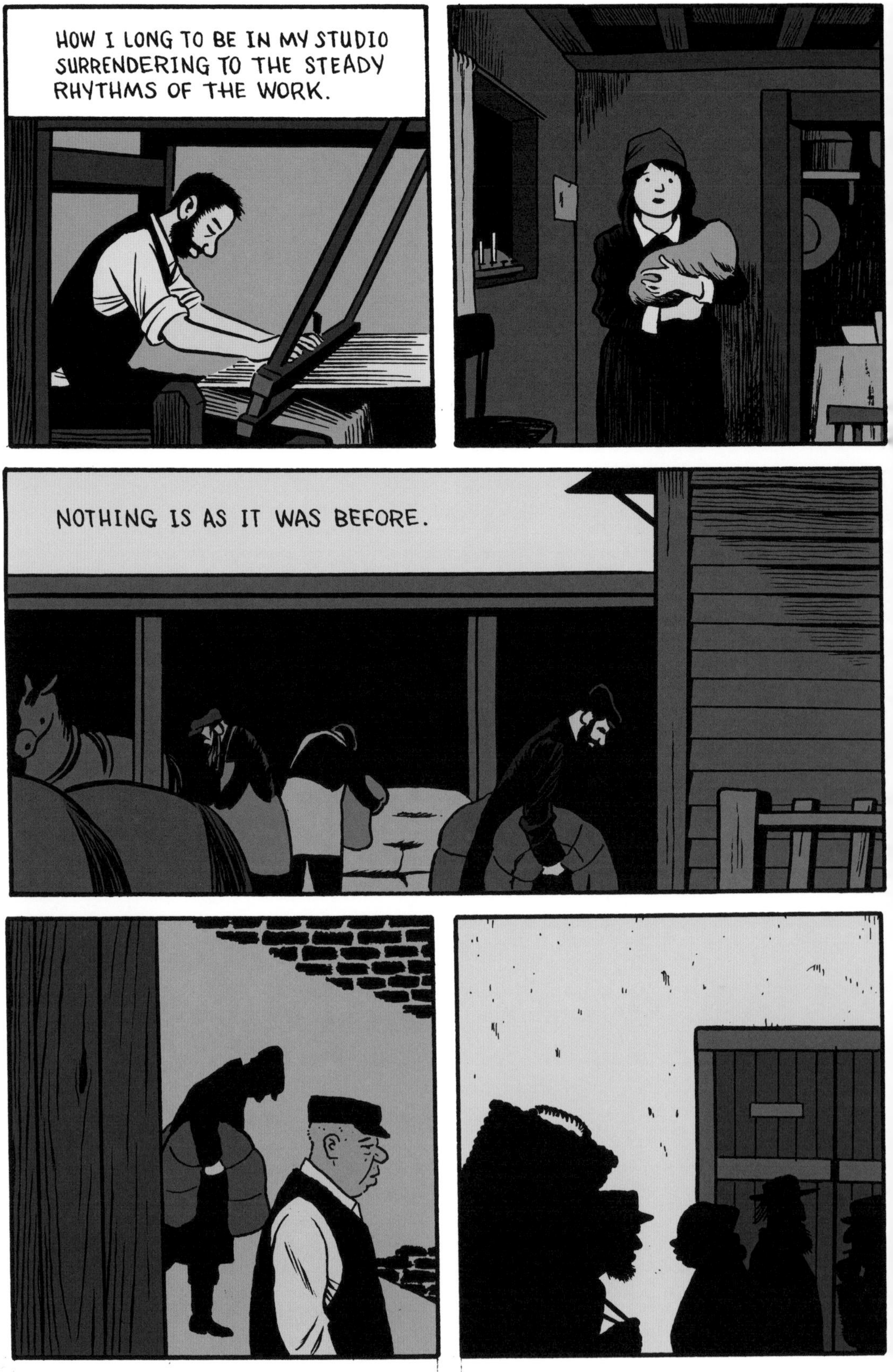
HOW I LONG TO BE IN MY STUDIO SURRENDERING TO THE STEADY RHYTHMS OF THE WORK.
NOTHING IS AS IT WAS BEFORE.

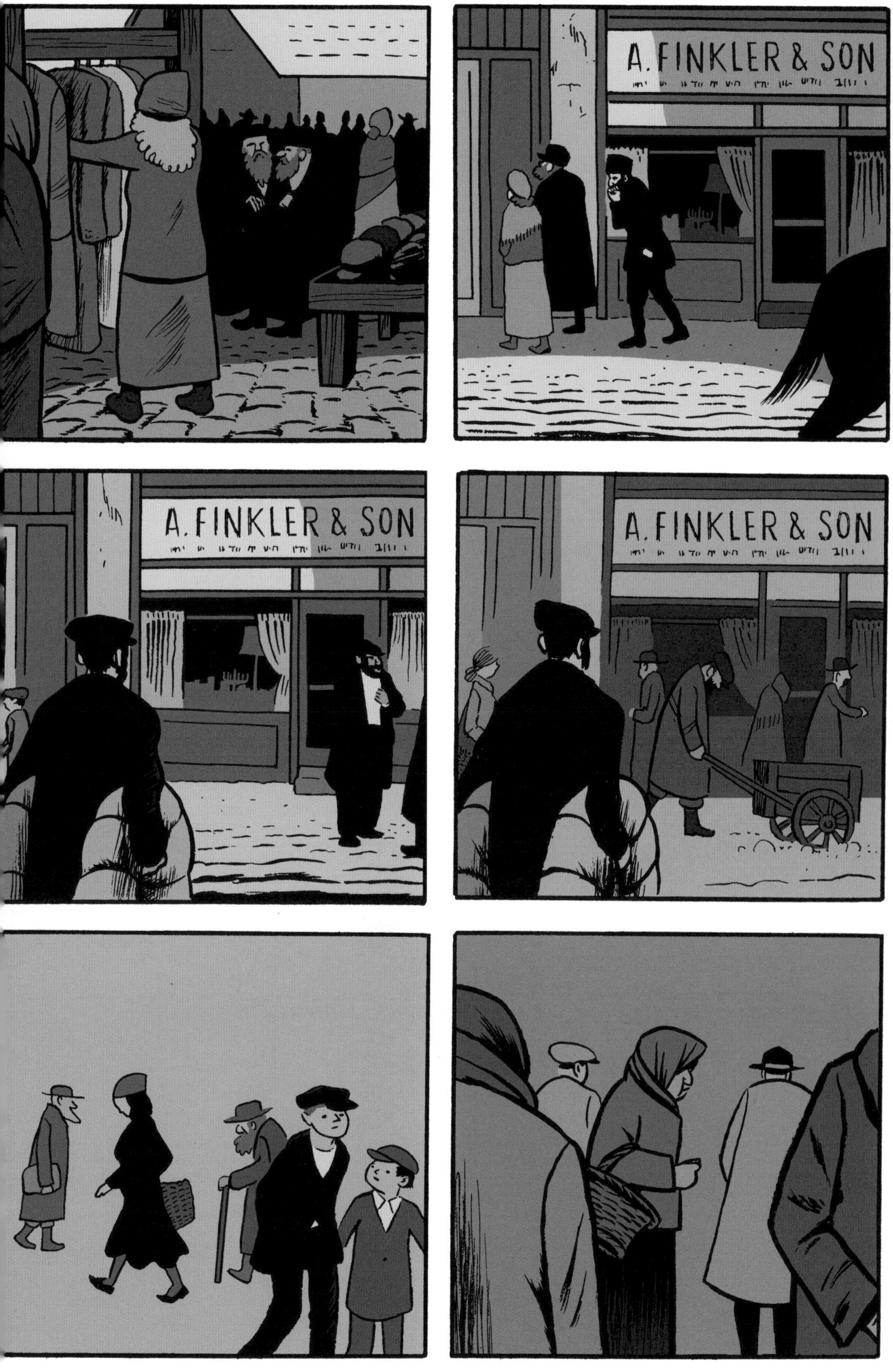
A. FINKLER & SON
A. FINKLER & SON
A. FINKLER & SON

UP AHEAD I SEE LEFF.

I HESITATE TO APPROACH HIM WHILE HE IS HOLDING COURT.

MY PRESENCE WOULD ONLY CAUSE DISCOMFORT...

LEFF!

AS MY COUNTENANCE HAS ALWAYS BETRAYED MY STATE OF MIND.

MENDLEMAN...!

GOD BLESS LEFF—HIS SELF-ASSURANCE AND GOOD NATURE MAKE HIM EASY TO CONFIDE IN. I SPEAK OF MY TROUBLES AND REMOVE THEIR STING.

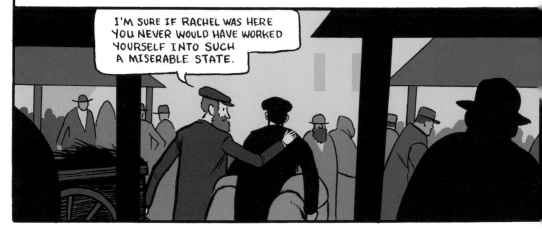

I'M SURE IF RACHEL WAS HERE YOU NEVER WOULD HAVE WORKED YOURSELF INTO SUCH A MISERABLE STATE.

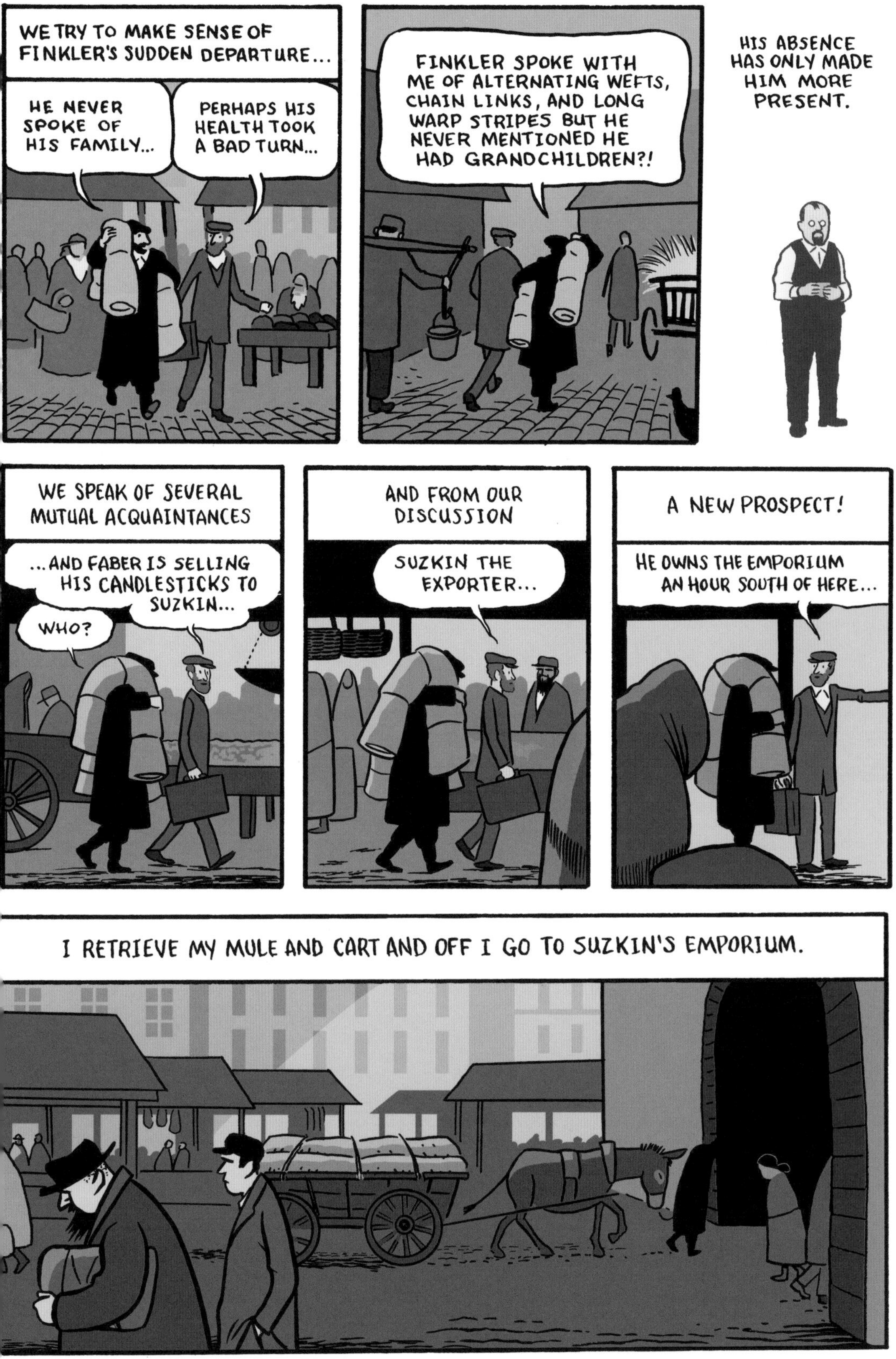
WE TRY TO MAKE SENSE OF FINKLER'S SUDDEN DEPARTURE...
HE NEVER SPOKE OF HIS FAMILY...
PERHAPS HIS HEALTH TOOK A BAD TURN...
FINKLER SPOKE WITH ME OF ALTERNATING WEFTS, CHAIN LINKS, AND LONG WARP STRIPES BUT HE NEVER MENTIONED HE HAD GRANDCHILDREN?!
HIS ABSENCE HAS ONLY MADE HIM MORE PRESENT.
WE SPEAK OF SEVERAL MUTUAL ACQUAINTANCES
...AND FABER IS SELLING HIS CANDLESTICKS TO SUZKIN...
WHO?
AND FROM OUR DISCUSSION
SUZKIN THE EXPORTER...
A NEW PROSPECT!
HE OWNS THE EMPORIUM AN HOUR SOUTH OF HERE...
I RETRIEVE MY MULE AND CART AND OFF I GO TO SUZKIN'S EMPORIUM.

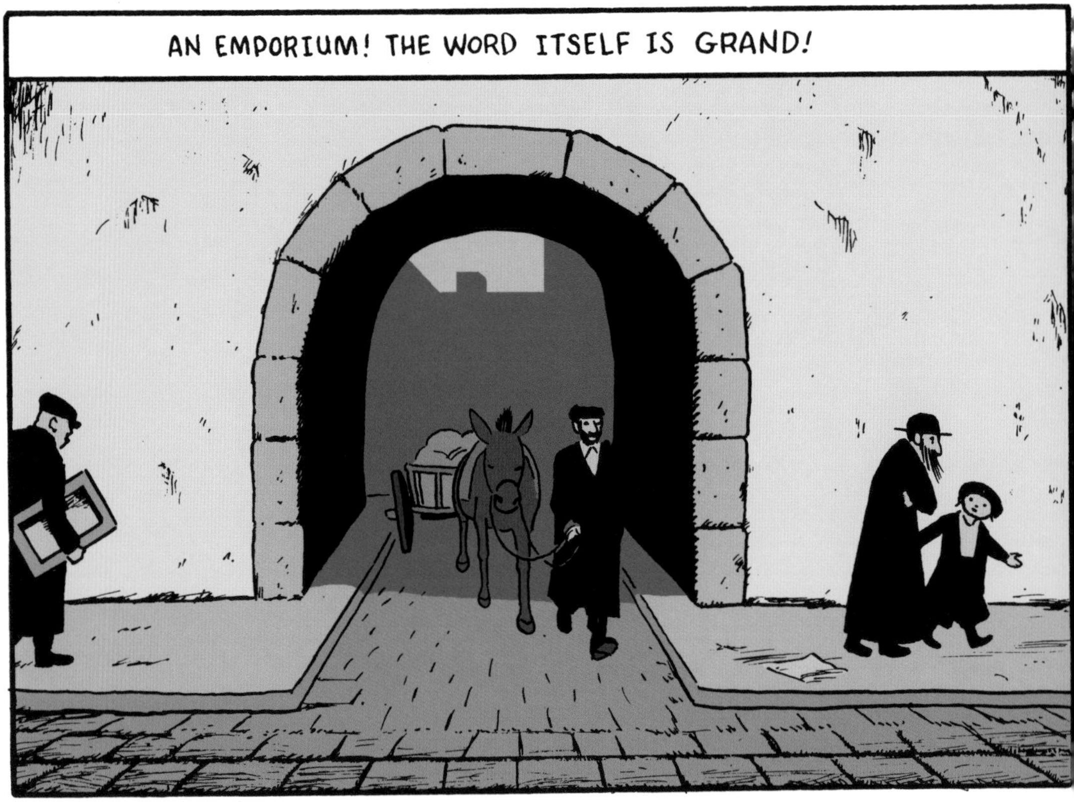
AN EMPORIUM! THE WORD ITSELF IS GRAND!

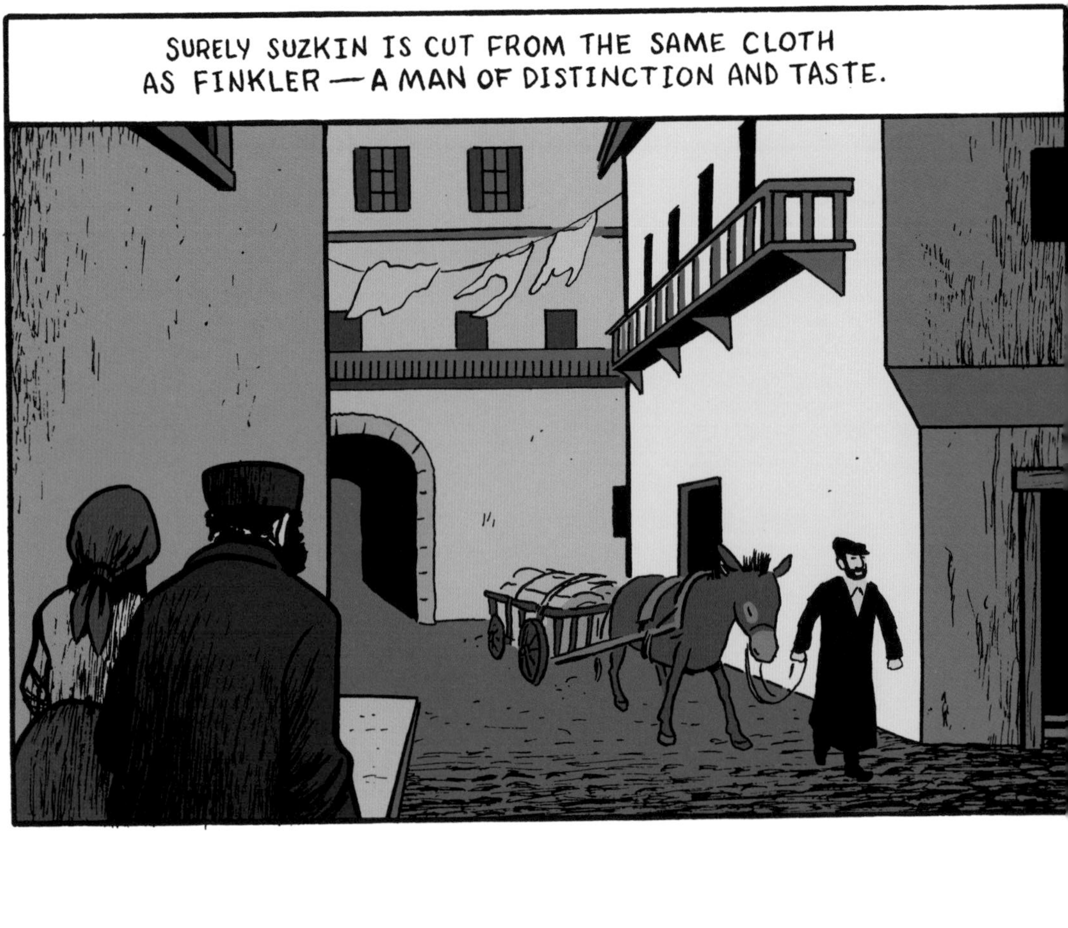
SURELY SUZKIN IS CUT FROM THE SAME CLOTH AS FINKLER — A MAN OF DISTINCTION AND TASTE.

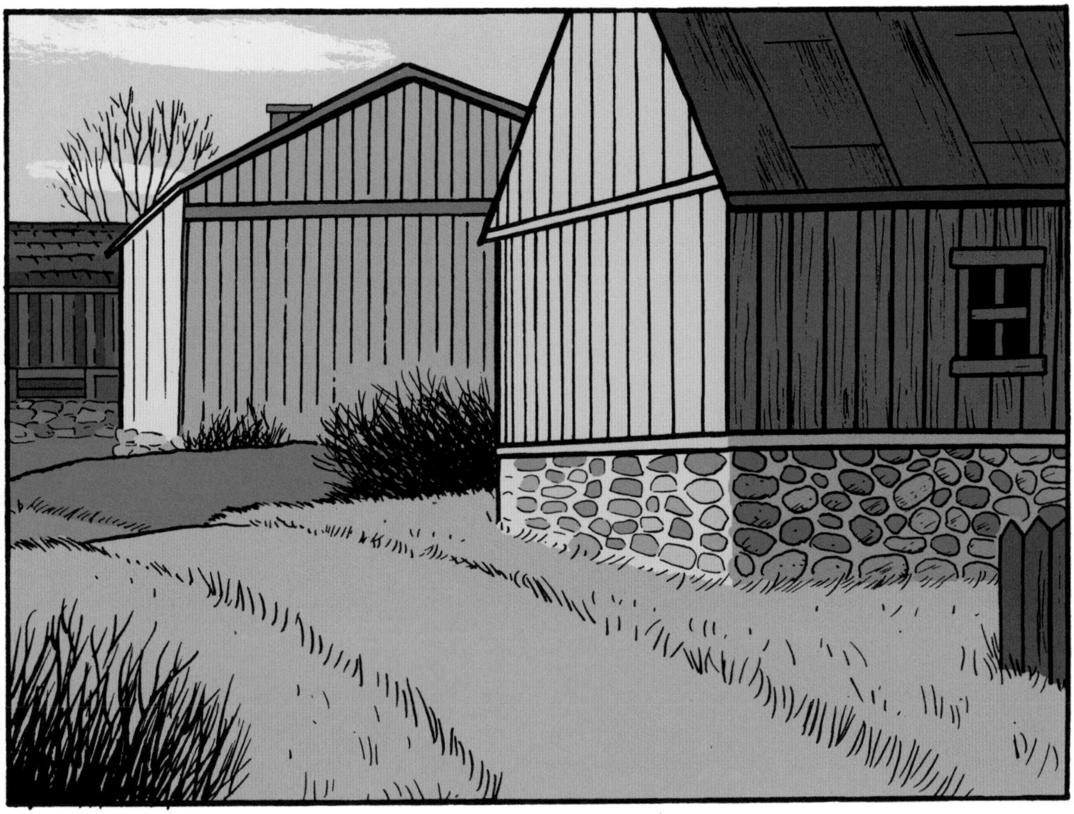
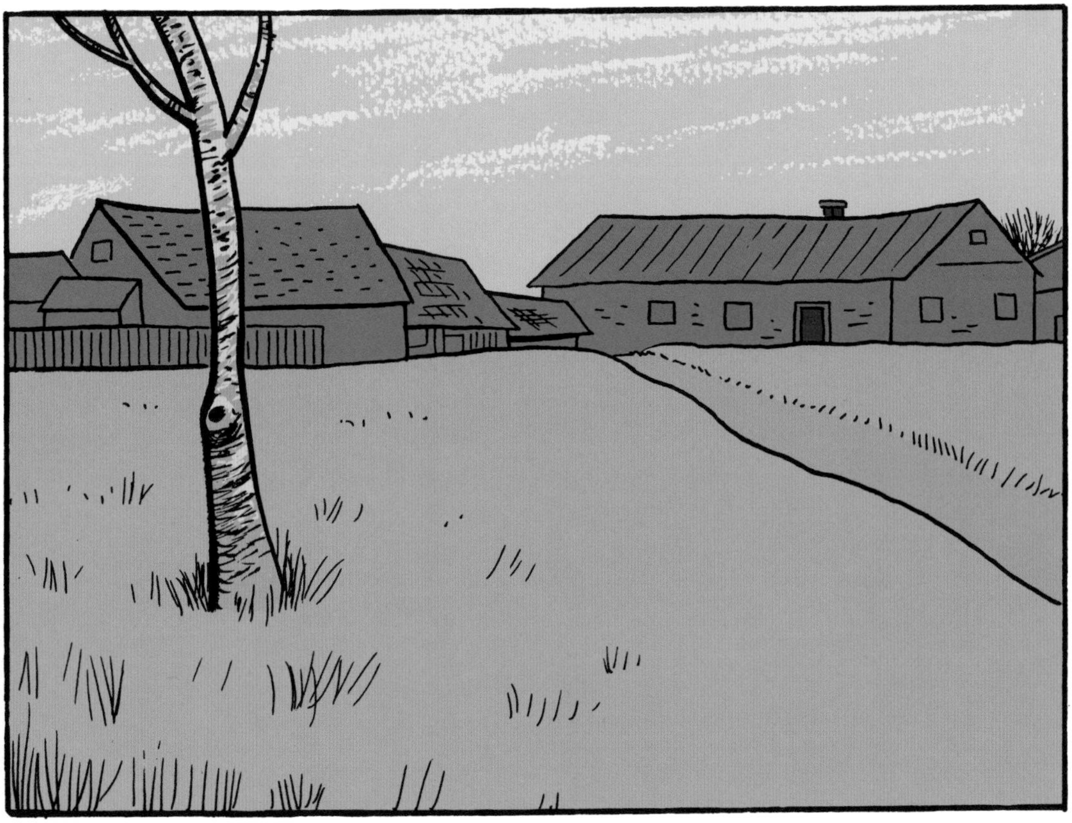

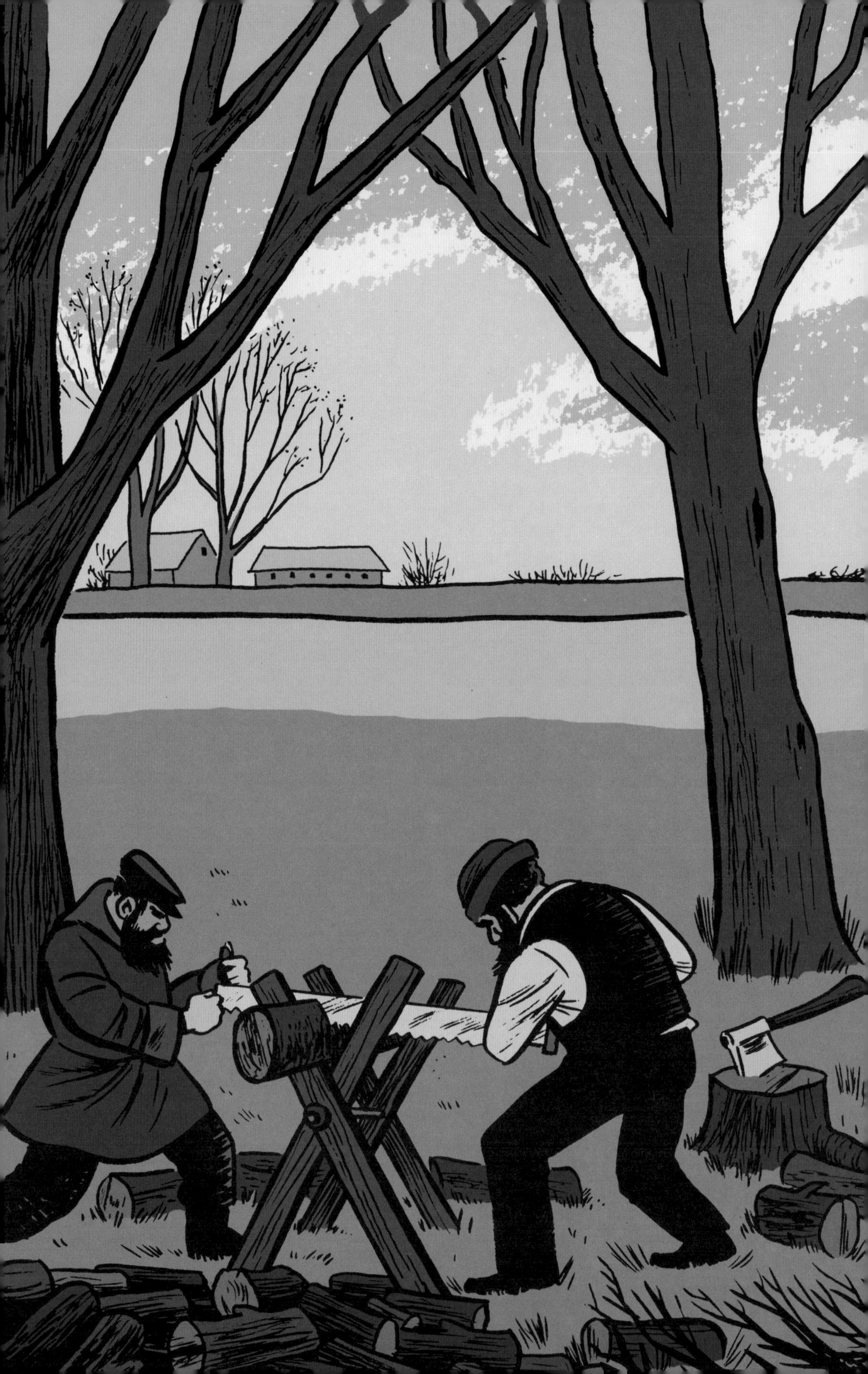

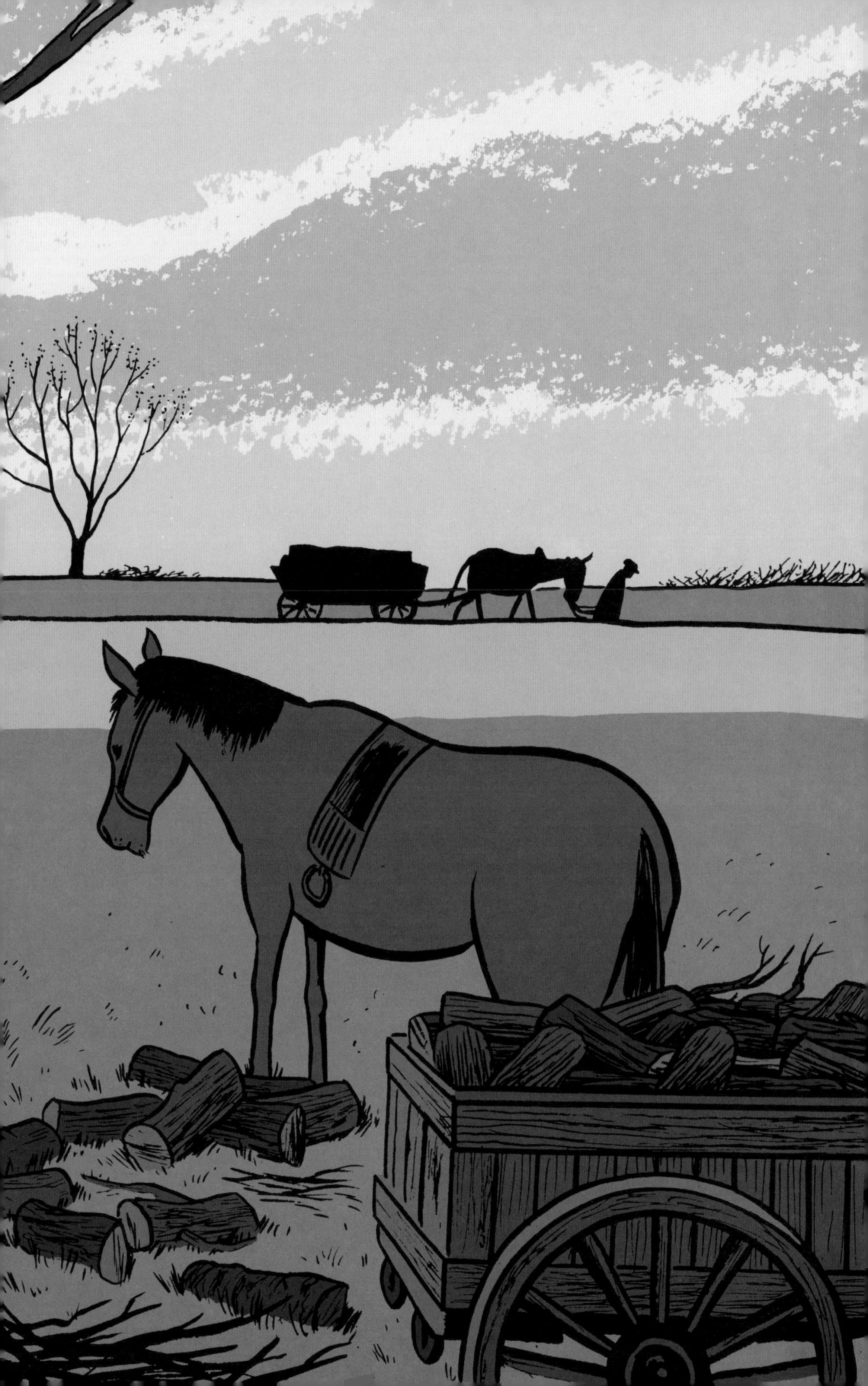

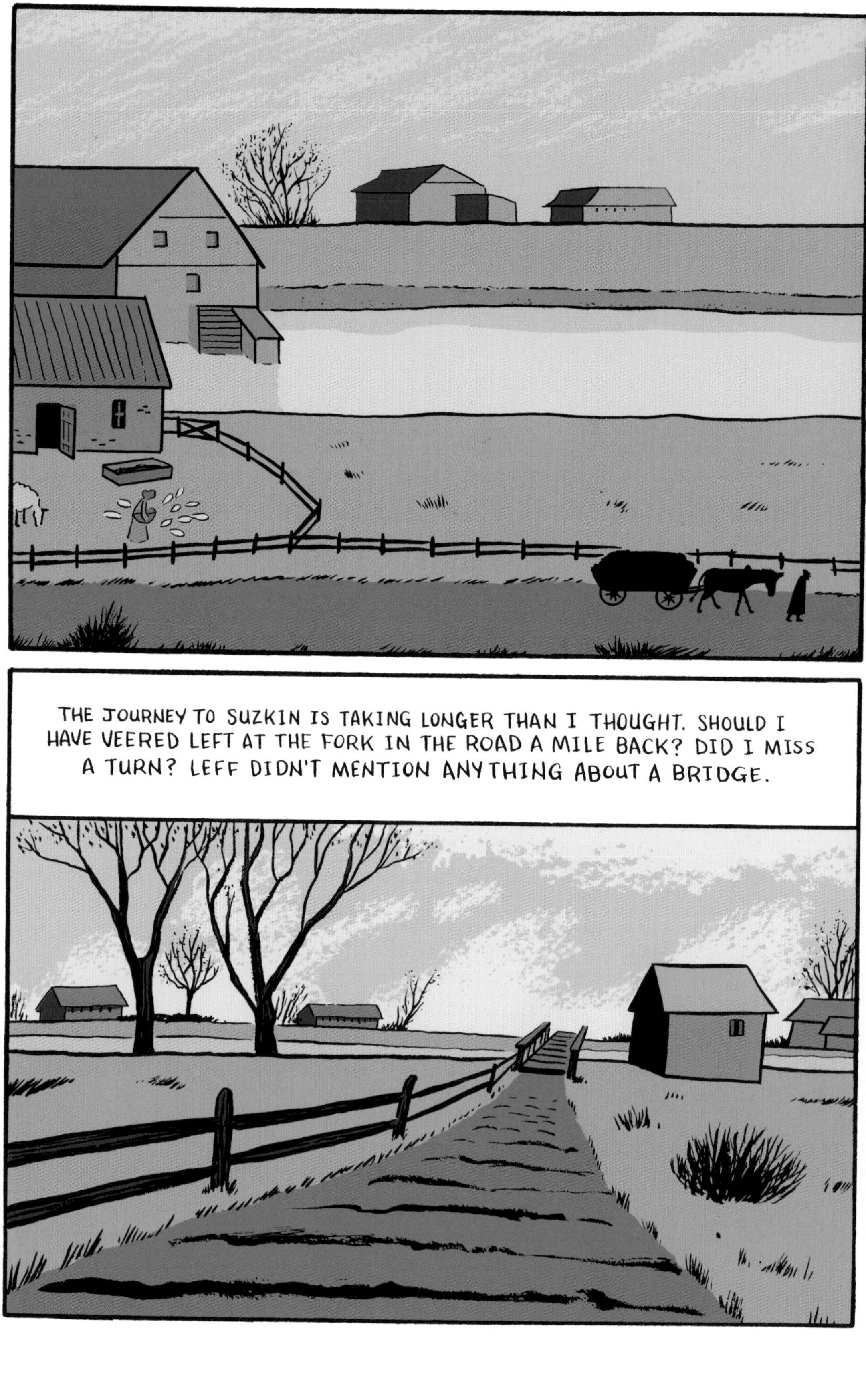
THE JOURNEY TO SUZKIN IS TAKING LONGER THAN I THOUGHT. SHOULD I HAVE VEERED LEFT AT THE FORK IN THE ROAD A MILE BACK? DID I MISS A TURN? LEFF DIDN'T MENTION ANYTHING ABOUT A BRIDGE.

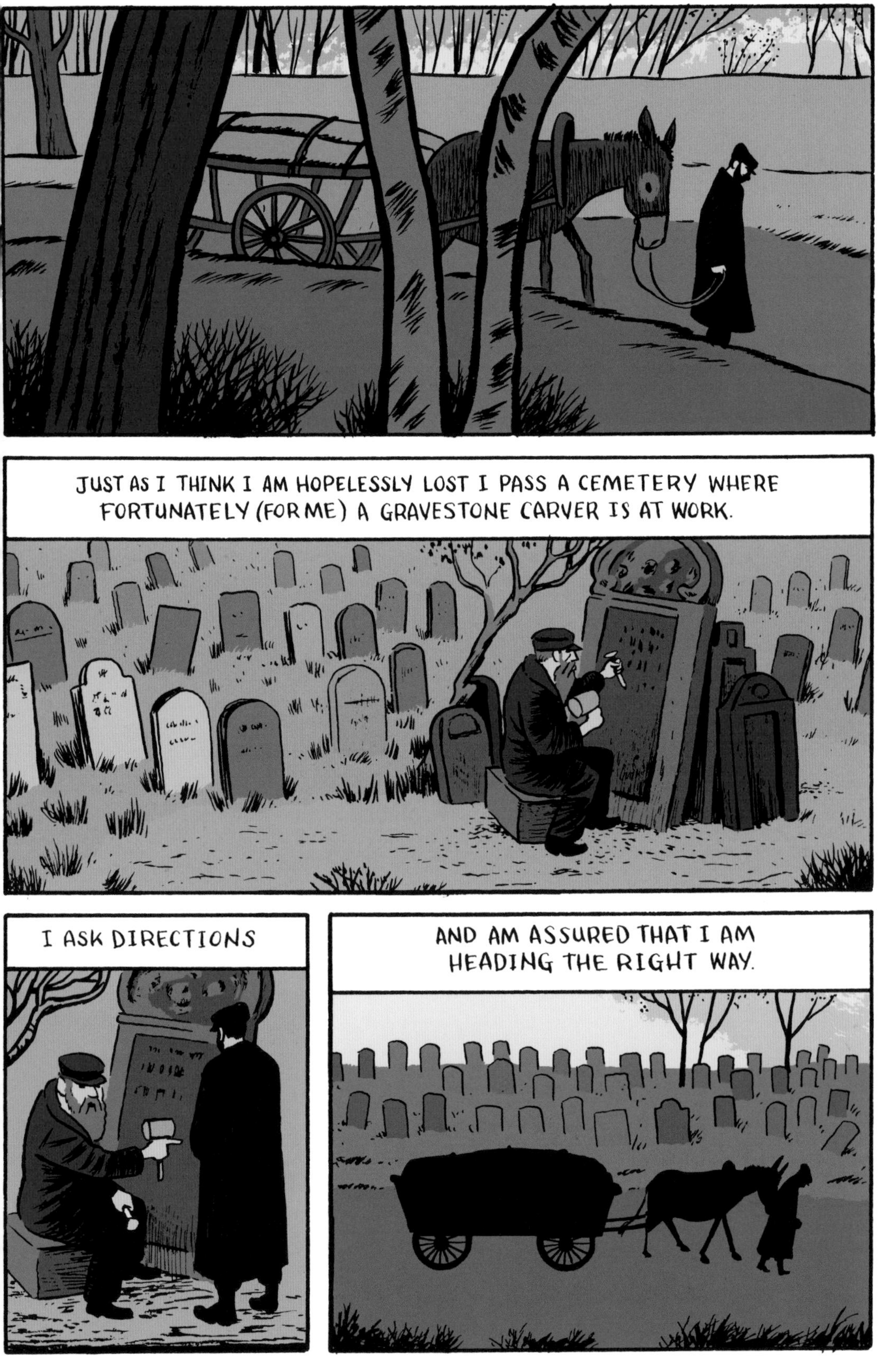
JUST AS I THINK I AM HOPELESSLY LOST I PASS A CEMETERY WHERE FORTUNATELY (FOR ME) A GRAVESTONE CARVER IS AT WORK.
I ASK DIRECTIONS
AND AM ASSURED THAT I AM HEADING THE RIGHT WAY.

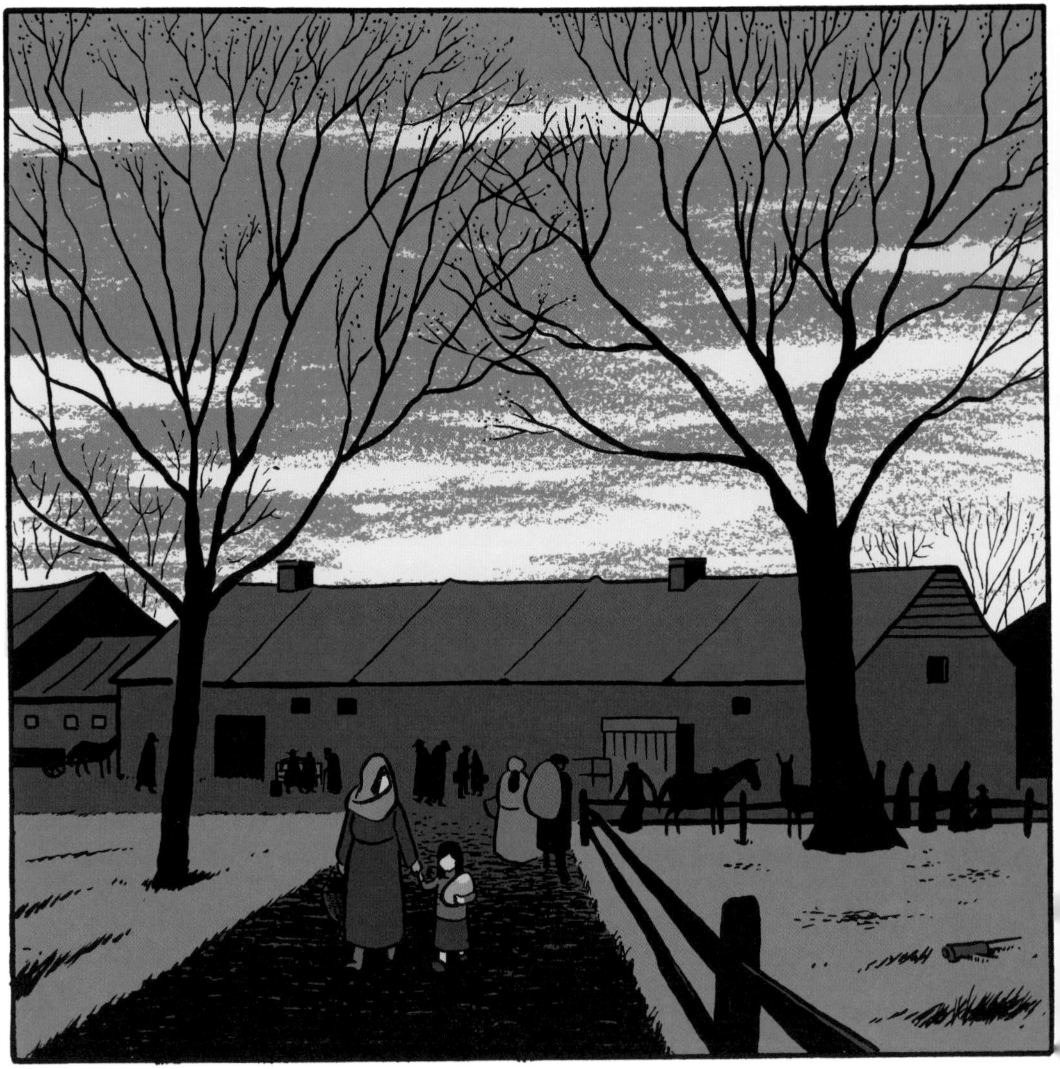

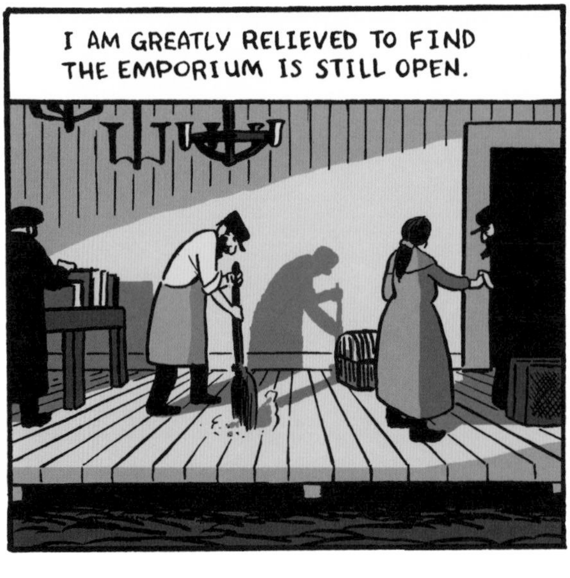
I AM GREATLY RELIEVED TO FIND THE EMPORIUM IS STILL OPEN.

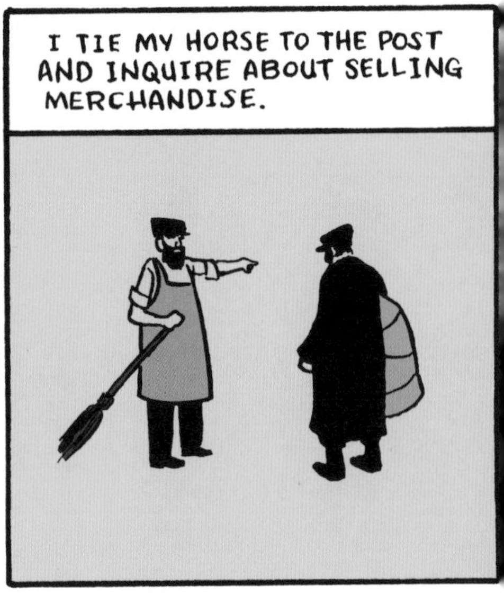
I TIE MY HORSE TO THE POST AND INQUIRE ABOUT SELLING MERCHANDISE.

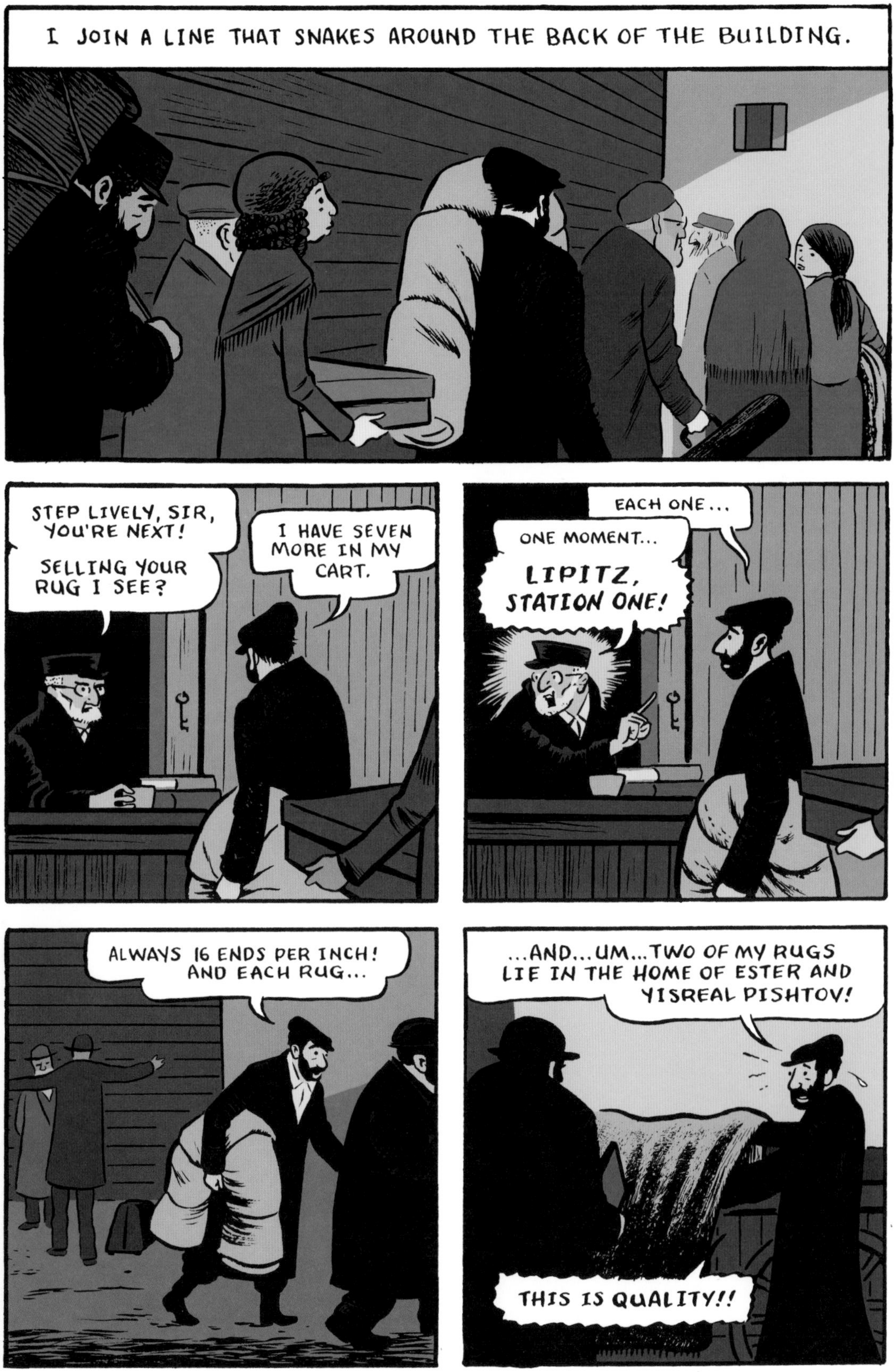
I JOIN A LINE THAT SNAKES AROUND THE BACK OF THE BUILDING.
STEP LIVELY, SIR, YOU'RE NEXT!
SELLING YOUR RUG I SEE?
I HAVE SEVEN MORE IN MY CART.
EACH ONE...
ONE MOMENT...
LIPITZ, STATION ONE!
ALWAYS 16 ENDS PER INCH! AND EACH RUG...
...AND...UM...TWO OF MY RUGS LIE IN THE HOME OF ESTER AND YISREAL PISHTOV!
THIS IS QUALITY!!

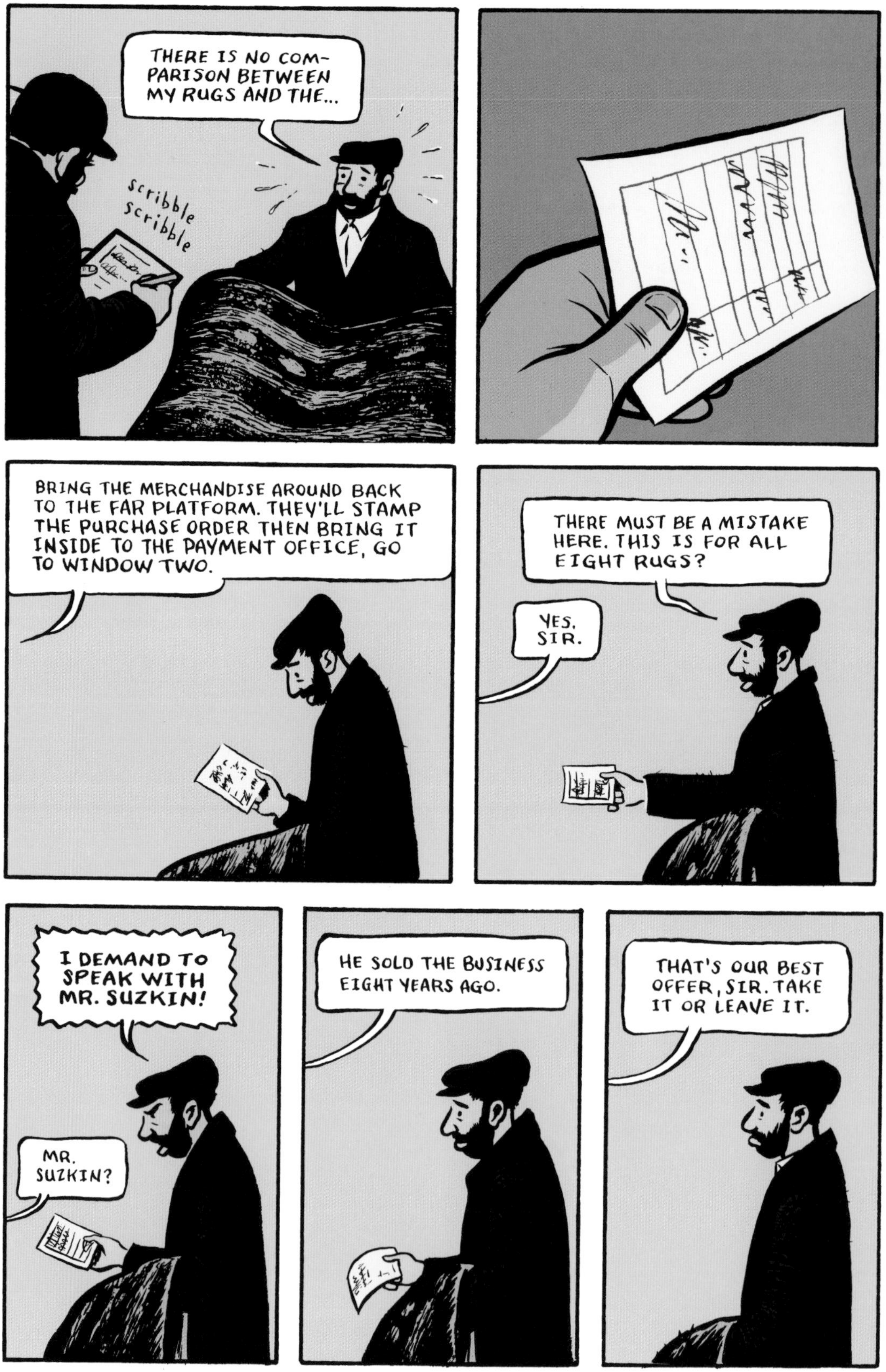
THERE IS NO COMPARISON BETWEEN MY RUGS AND THE...
scribble scribble
BRING THE MERCHANDISE AROUND BACK TO THE FAR PLATFORM. THEY'LL STAMP THE PURCHASE ORDER THEN BRING IT INSIDE TO THE PAYMENT OFFICE, GO TO WINDOW TWO.
THERE MUST BE A MISTAKE HERE. THIS IS FOR ALL EIGHT RUGS?
YES, SIR.
I DEMAND TO SPEAK WITH MR. SUZKIN!
MR. SUZKIN?
HE SOLD THE BUSINESS EIGHT YEARS AGO.
THAT'S OUR BEST OFFER, SIR. TAKE IT OR LEAVE IT.

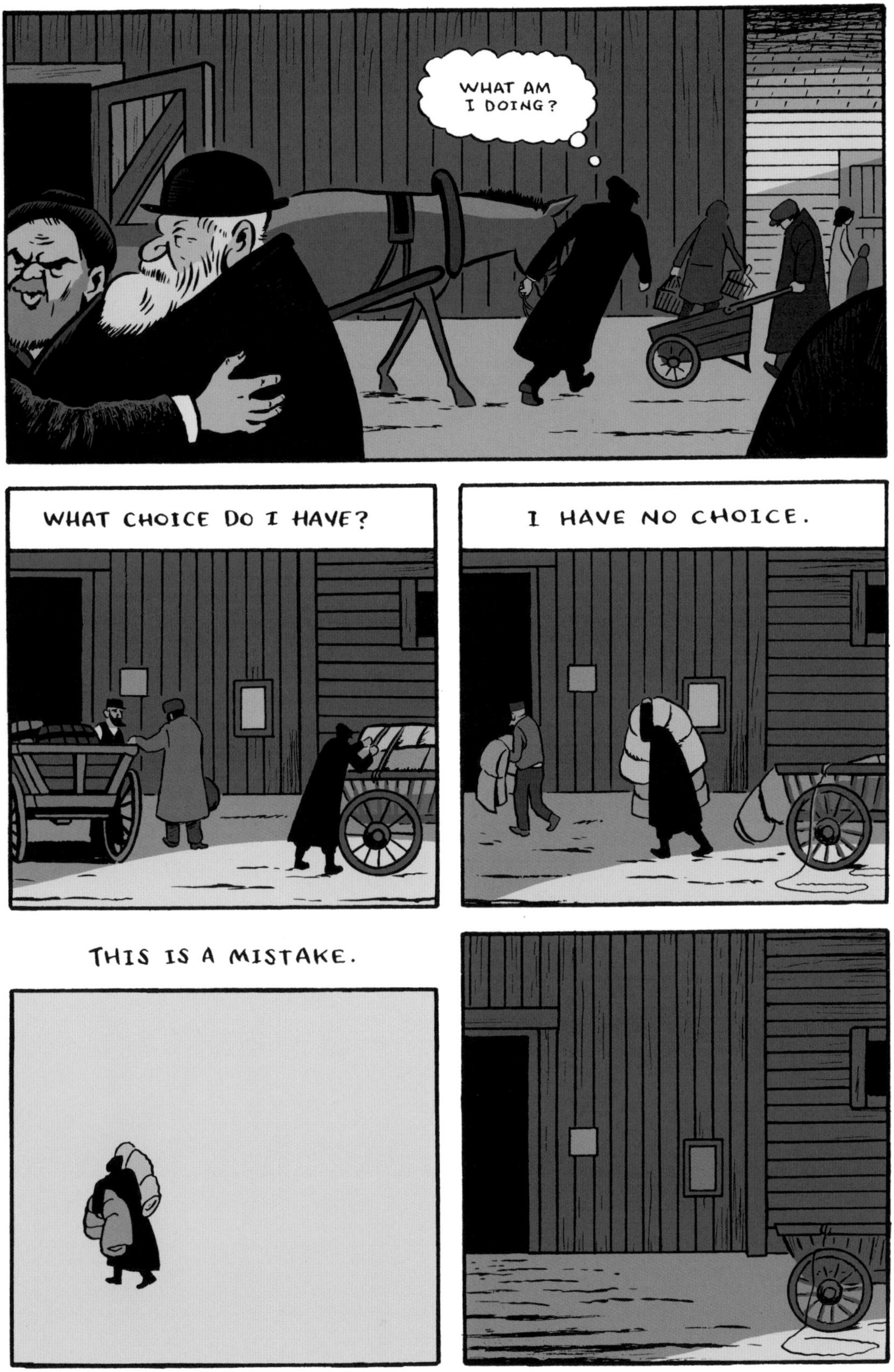
WHAT AM I DOING?
WHAT CHOICE DO I HAVE?
I HAVE NO CHOICE.
THIS IS A MISTAKE.

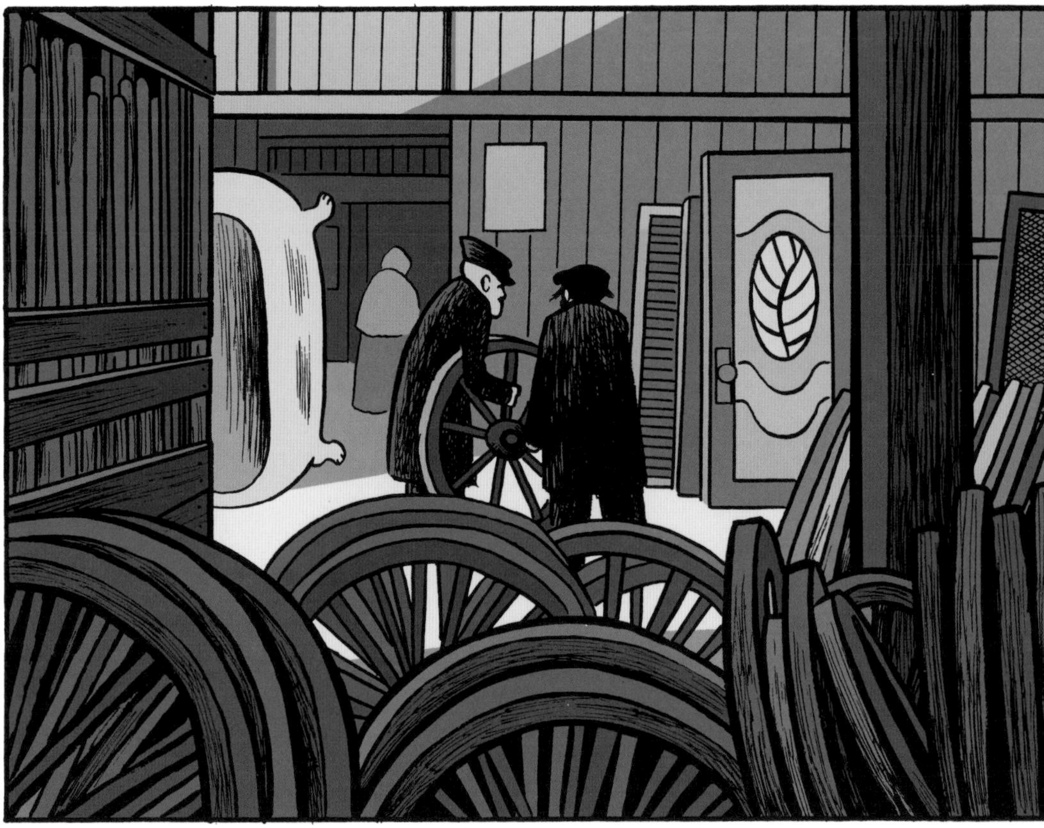

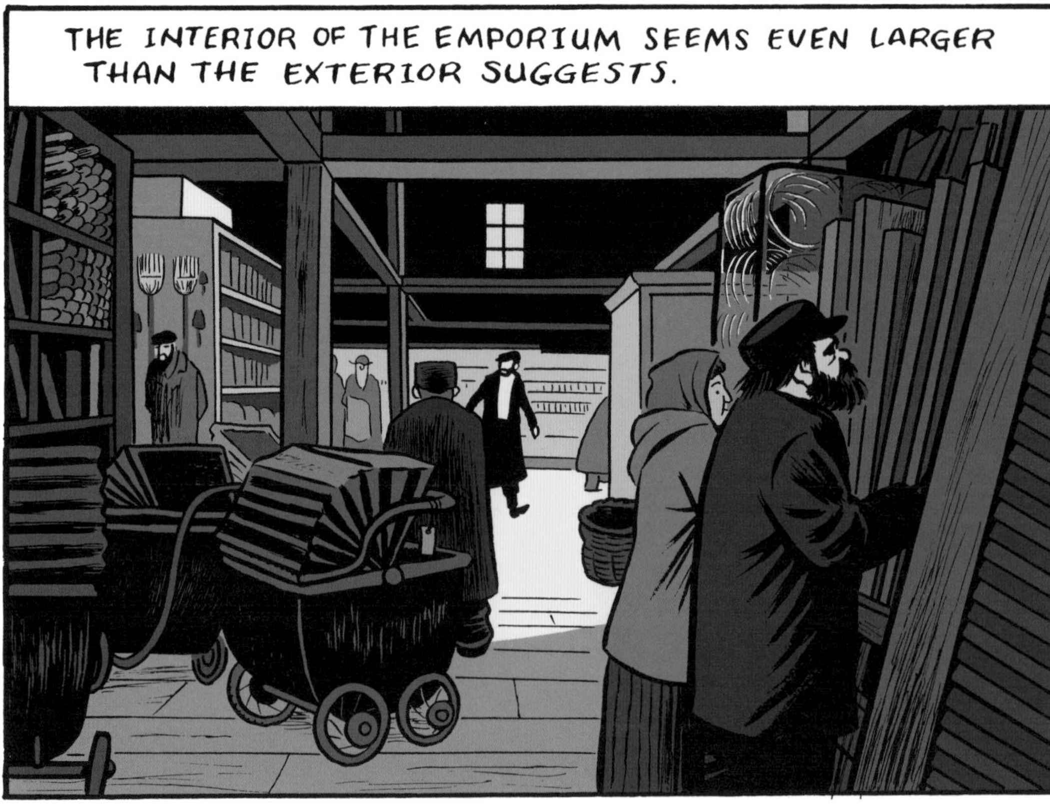
THE INTERIOR OF THE EMPORIUM SEEMS EVEN LARGER THAN THE EXTERIOR SUGGESTS.

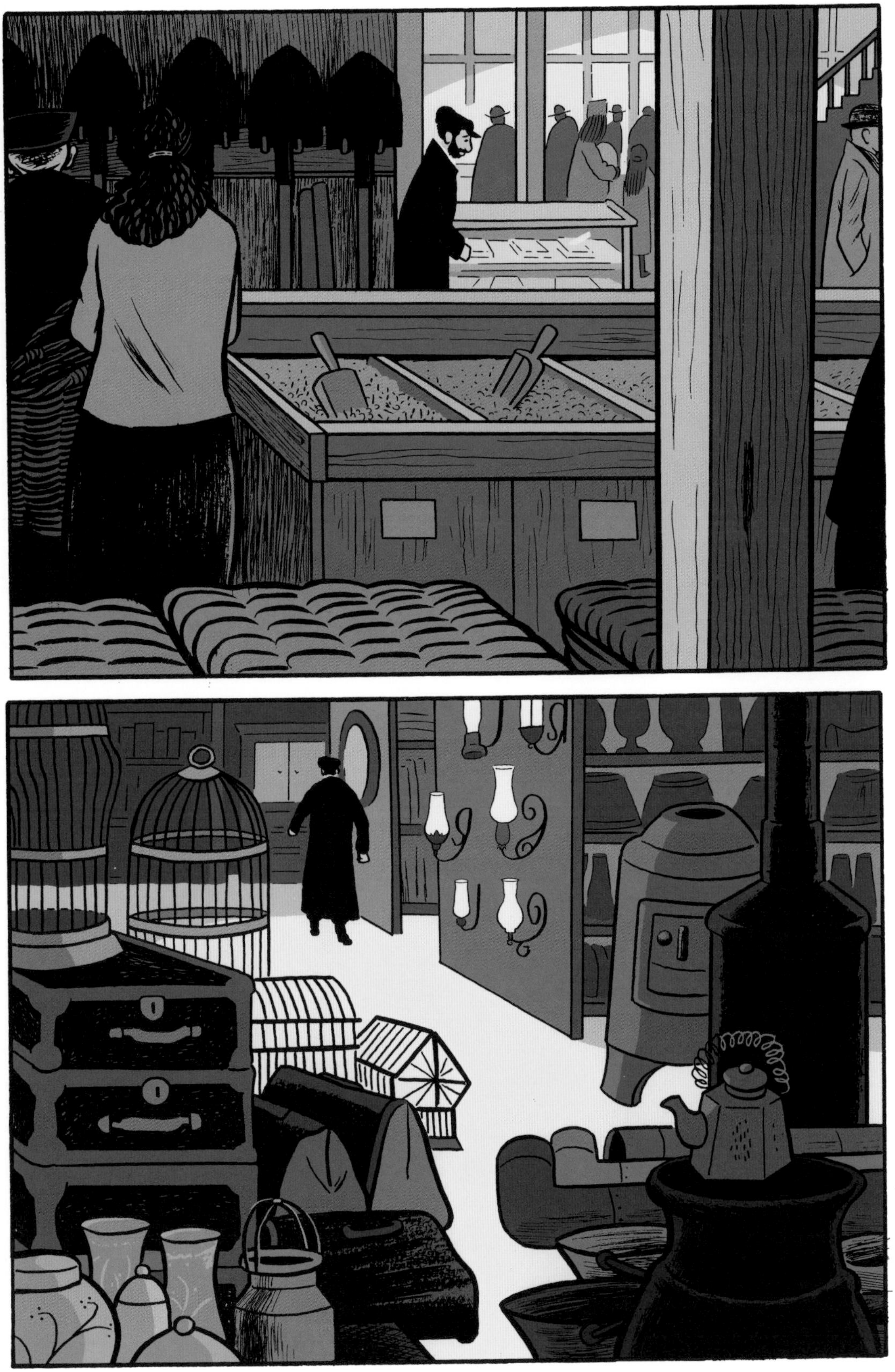

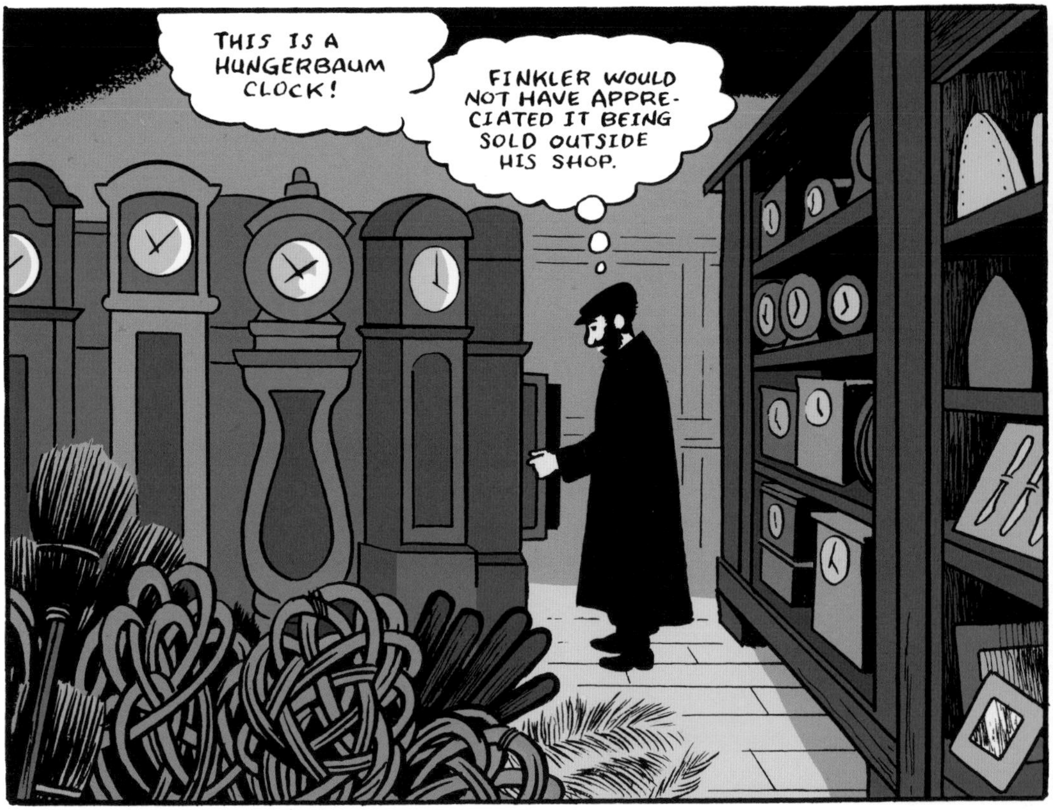
THIS IS A HUNGERBAUM CLOCK!
FINKLER WOULD NOT HAVE APPRECIATED IT BEING SOLD OUTSIDE HIS SHOP.

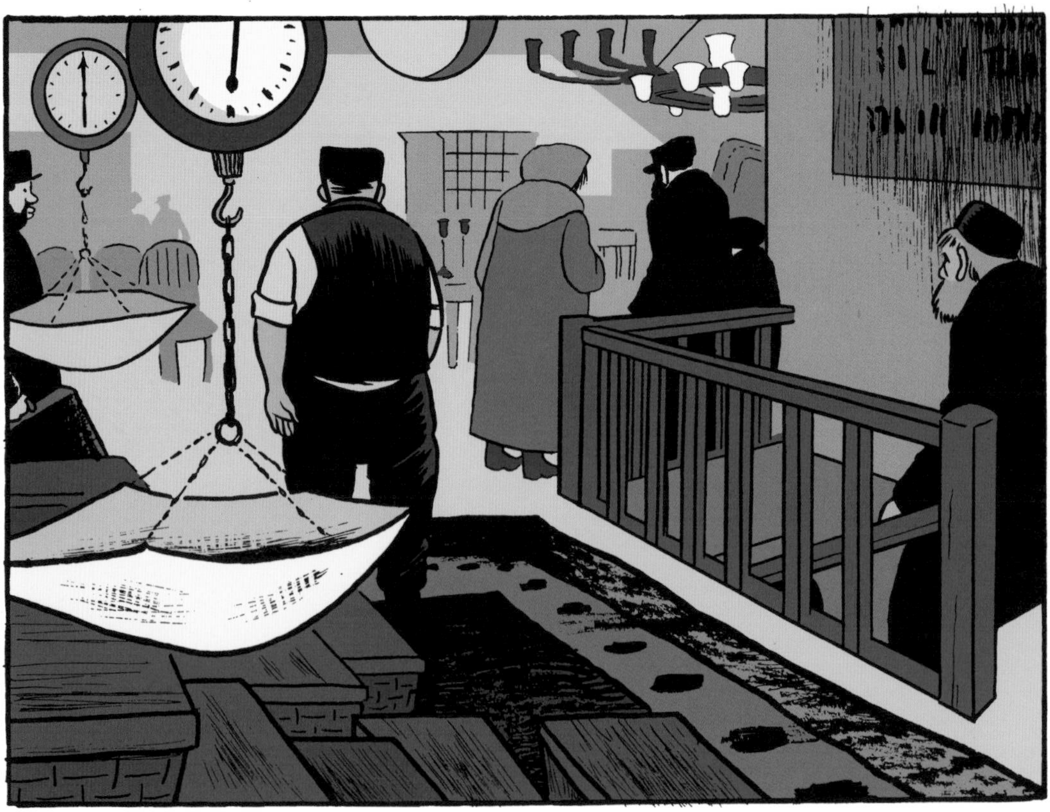

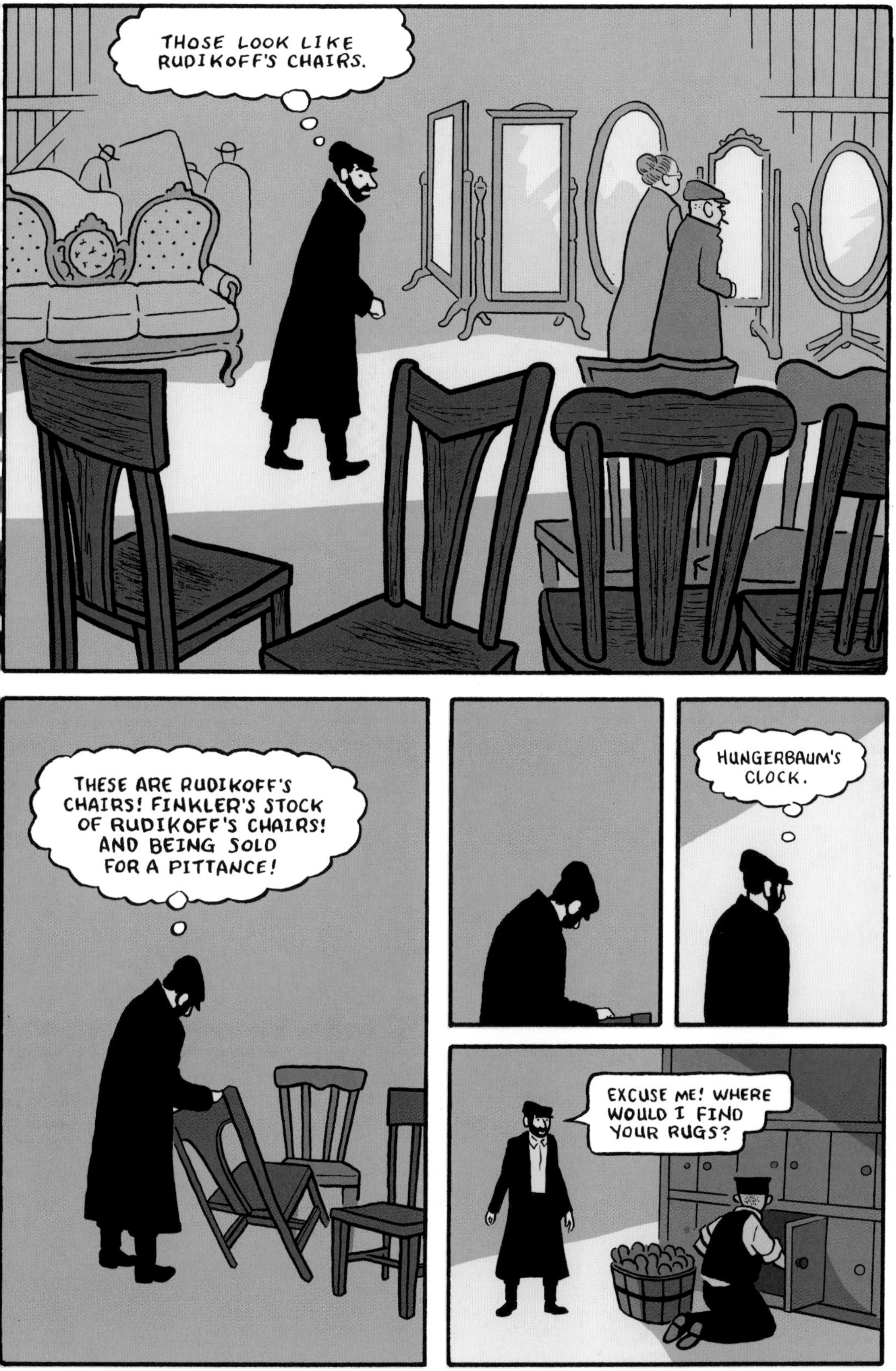
THOSE LOOK LIKE RUDIKOFF'S CHAIRS.
THESE ARE RUDIKOFF'S CHAIRS! FINKLER'S STOCK OF RUDIKOFF'S CHAIRS! AND BEING SOLD FOR A PITTANCE!
HUNGERBAUM'S CLOCK.
EXCUSE ME! WHERE WOULD I FIND YOUR RUGS?

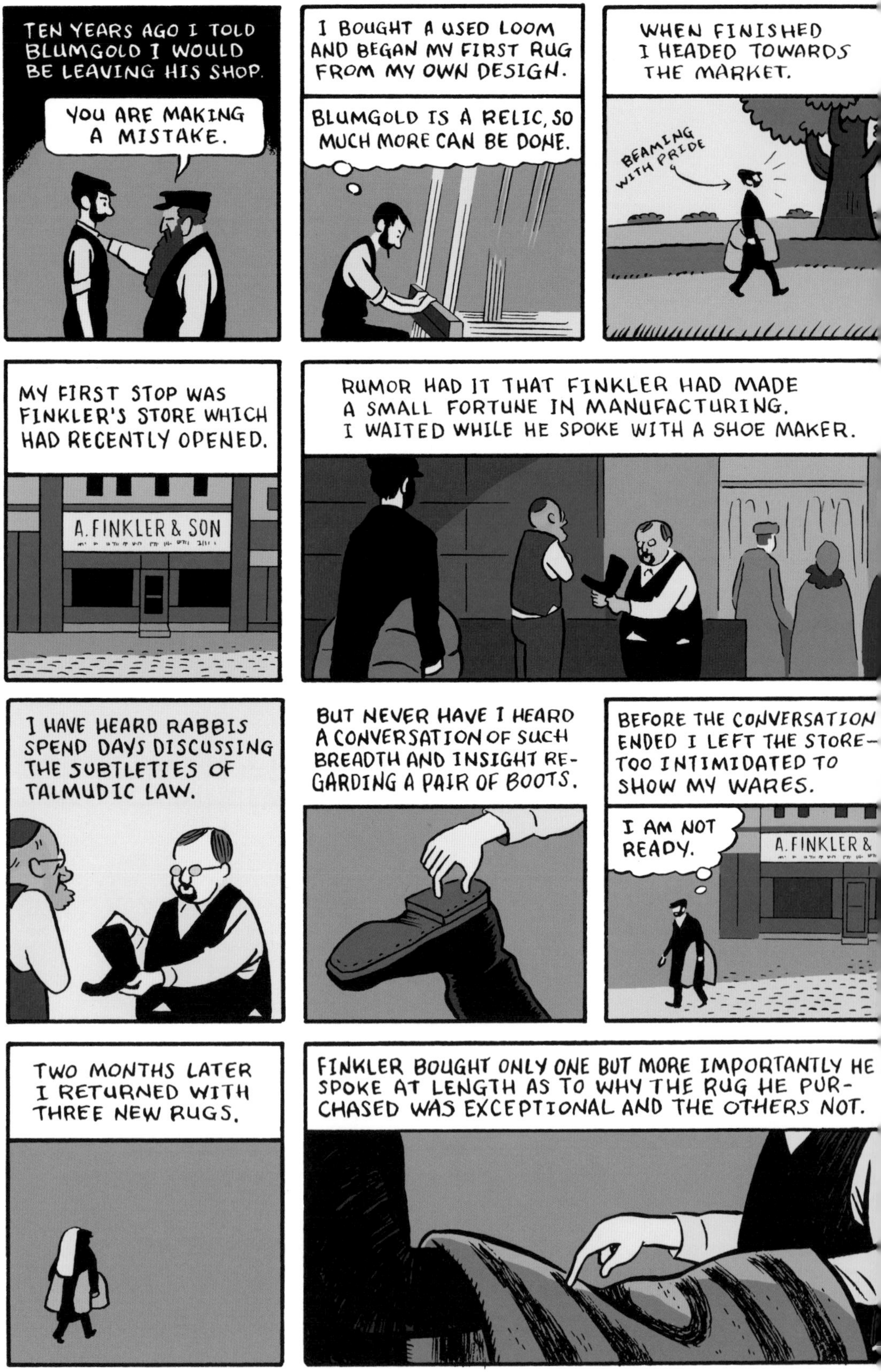
TEN YEARS AGO I TOLD BLUMGOLD I WOULD BE LEAVING HIS SHOP.
YOU ARE MAKING A MISTAKE.
I BOUGHT A USED LOOM AND BEGAN MY FIRST RUG FROM MY OWN DESIGN.
BLUMGOLD IS A RELIC, SO MUCH MORE CAN BE DONE.
WHEN FINISHED I HEADED TOWARDS THE MARKET.
BEAMING WITH PRIDE
MY FIRST STOP WAS FINKLER'S STORE WHICH HAD RECENTLY OPENED.
A. FINKLER & SON
RUMOR HAD IT THAT FINKLER HAD MADE A SMALL FORTUNE IN MANUFACTURING. I WAITED WHILE HE SPOKE WITH A SHOE MAKER.
I HAVE HEARD RABBIS SPEND DAYS DISCUSSING THE SUBTLETIES OF TALMUDIC LAW.
BUT NEVER HAVE I HEARD A CONVERSATION OF SUCH BREADTH AND INSIGHT REGARDING A PAIR OF BOOTS.
BEFORE THE CONVERSATION ENDED I LEFT THE STORE— TOO INTIMIDATED TO SHOW MY WARES.
I AM NOT READY.
A. FINKLER &
TWO MONTHS LATER I RETURNED WITH THREE NEW RUGS.
FINKLER BOUGHT ONLY ONE BUT MORE IMPORTANTLY HE SPOKE AT LENGTH AS TO WHY THE RUG HE PURCHASED WAS EXCEPTIONAL AND THE OTHERS NOT.

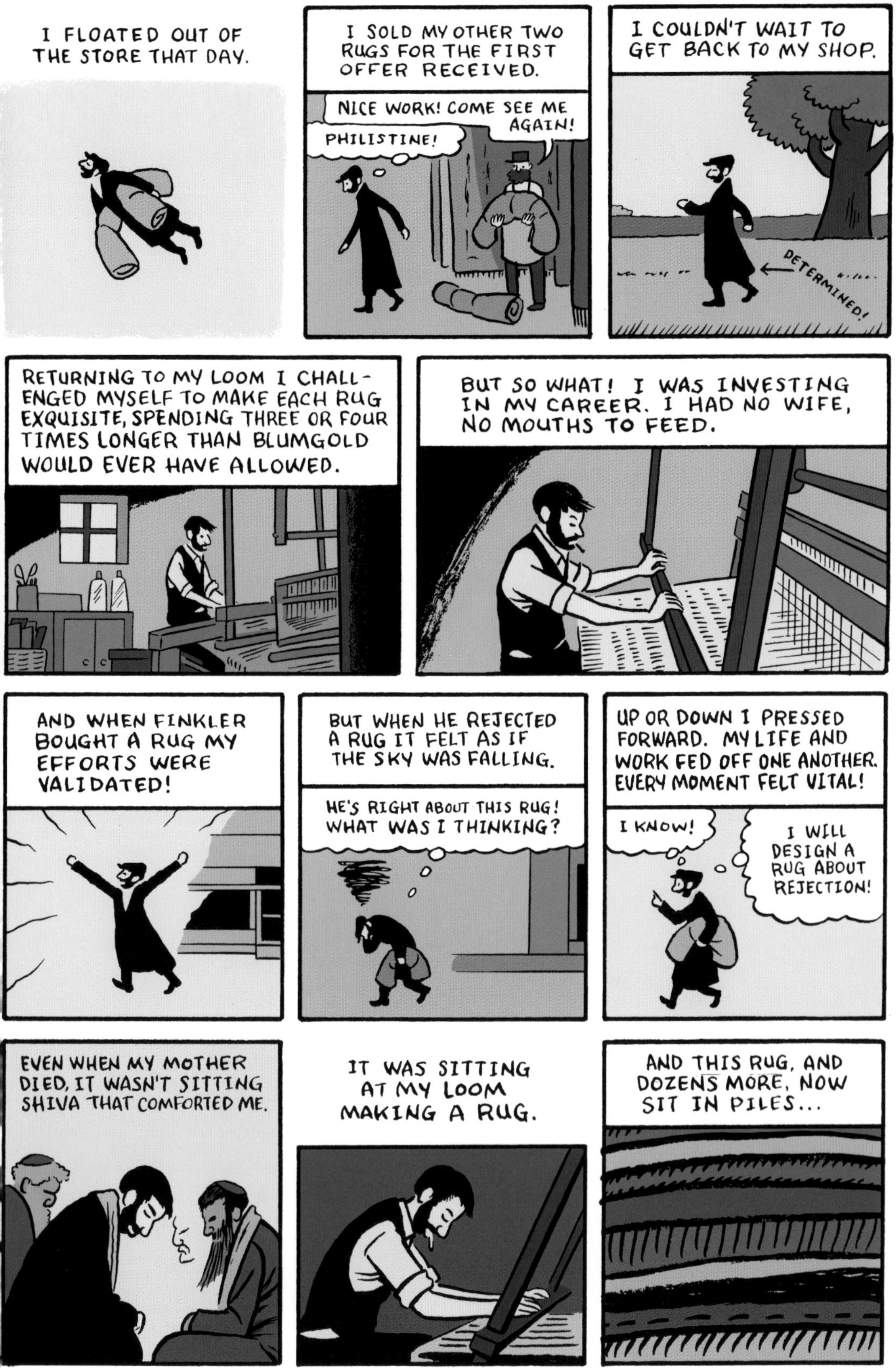
I FLOATED OUT OF THE STORE THAT DAY.
I SOLD MY OTHER TWO RUGS FOR THE FIRST OFFER RECEIVED.
NICE WORK! COME SEE ME AGAIN!
PHILISTINE!
I COULDN'T WAIT TO GET BACK TO MY SHOP.
DETERMINED!
RETURNING TO MY LOOM I CHALLENGED MYSELF TO MAKE EACH RUG EXQUISITE, SPENDING THREE OR FOUR TIMES LONGER THAN BLUMGOLD WOULD EVER HAVE ALLOWED.
BUT SO WHAT! I WAS INVESTING IN MY CAREER. I HAD NO WIFE, NO MOUTHS TO FEED.
AND WHEN FINKLER BOUGHT A RUG MY EFFORTS WERE VALIDATED!
BUT WHEN HE REJECTED A RUG IT FELT AS IF THE SKY WAS FALLING.
HE'S RIGHT ABOUT THIS RUG! WHAT WAS I THINKING?
UP OR DOWN I PRESSED FORWARD. MY LIFE AND WORK FED OFF ONE ANOTHER. EVERY MOMENT FELT VITAL!
I KNOW!
I WILL DESIGN A RUG ABOUT REJECTION!
EVEN WHEN MY MOTHER DIED, IT WASN'T SITTING SHIVA THAT COMFORTED ME.
IT WAS SITTING AT MY LOOM MAKING A RUG.
AND THIS RUG, AND DOZENS MORE, NOW SIT IN PILES...

A MONUMENT OF... OF WHAT? FAILURE? SELF-DELUSION?

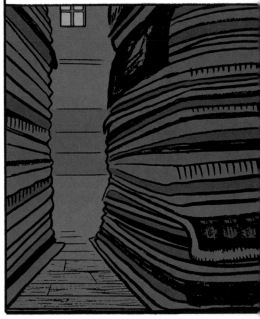

ALBERT FINKLER ENCOURAGED ME TO BUILD A HOUSE OF CARDS. MAY I NEVER HEAR OR SPEAK HIS NAME AGAIN.

OUTSIDE I REJOIN THE LINE.

YES SIR?

SELLING MY WAGON. AND A MULE IF YOU'LL TAKE IT...

YOU CAN TAKE THIS RIGHT TO THE PAYMENT OFFICE. IT WILL BE CLOSING SOON.

...FORTY-ONE, FORTY-TWO...

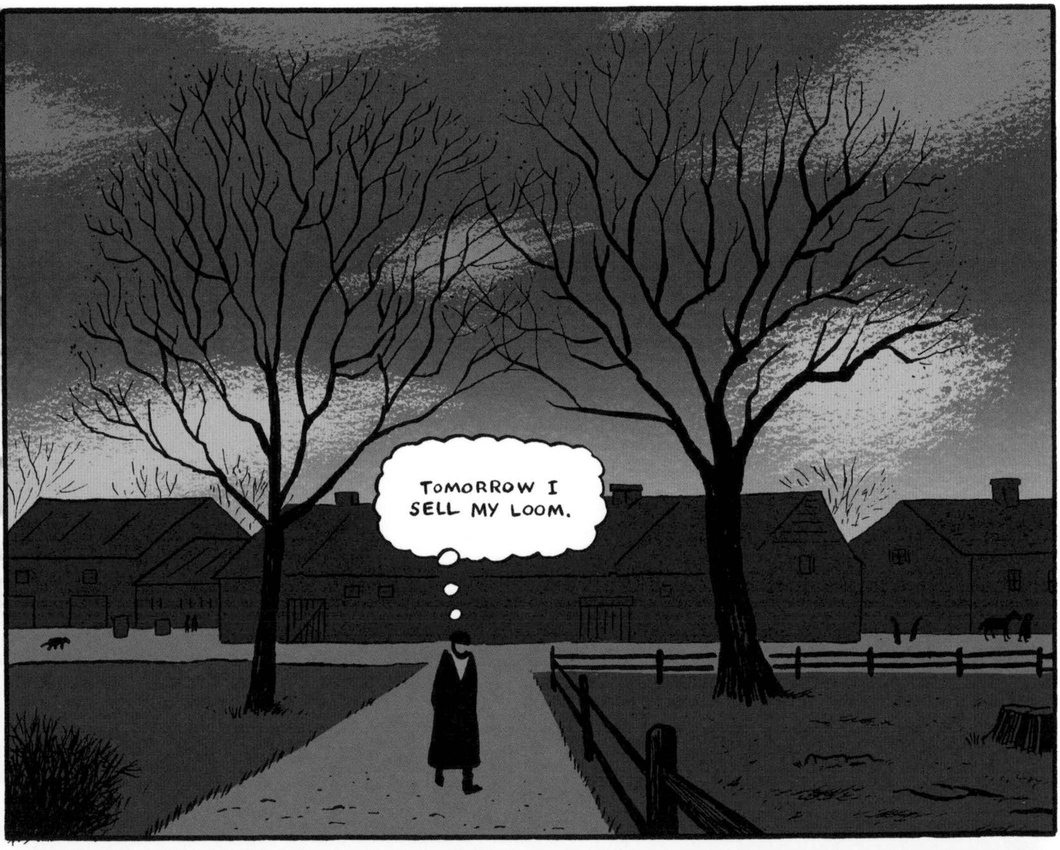
TOMORROW I SELL MY LOOM.

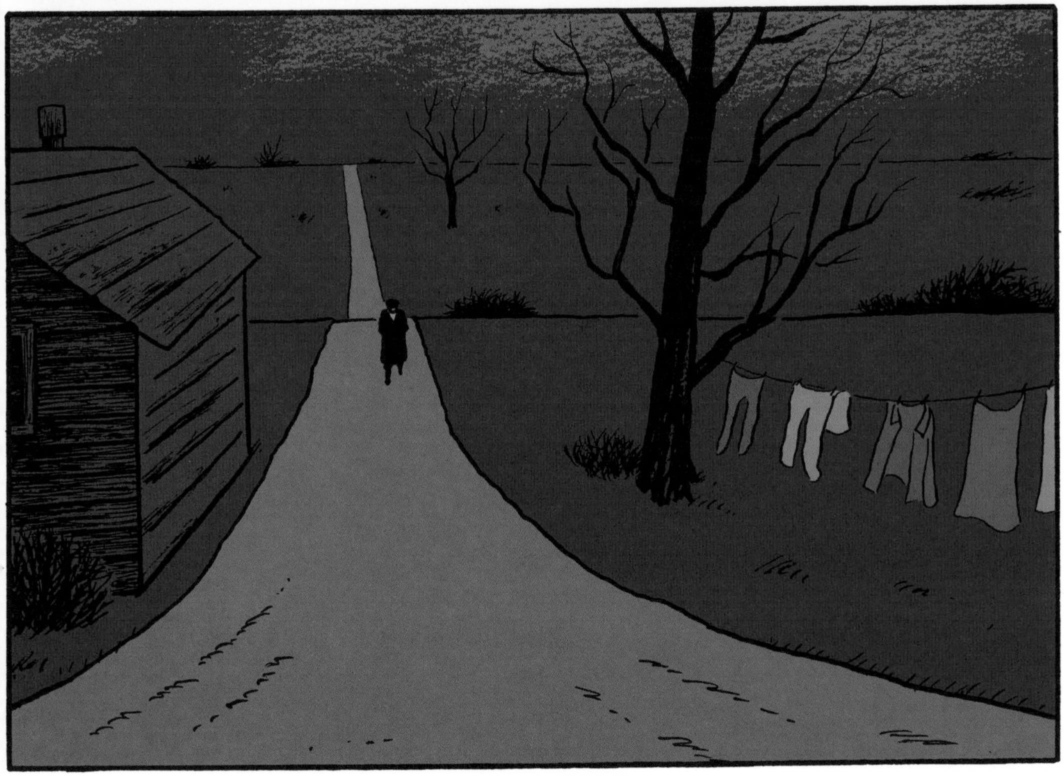

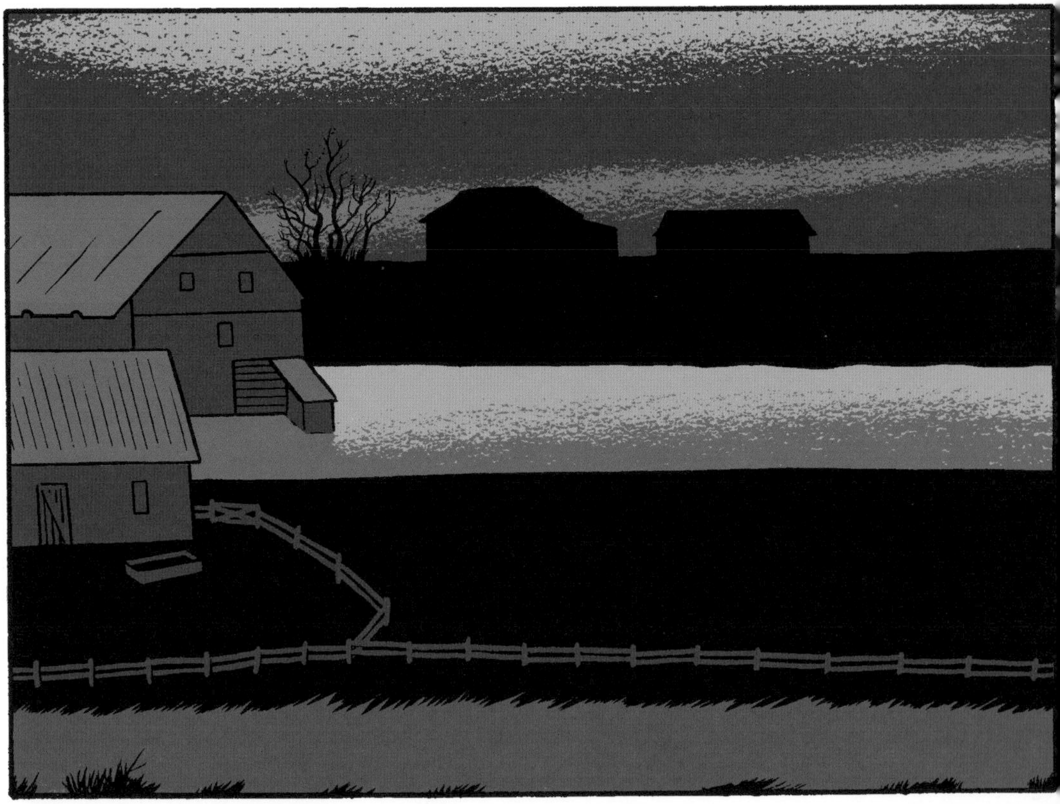

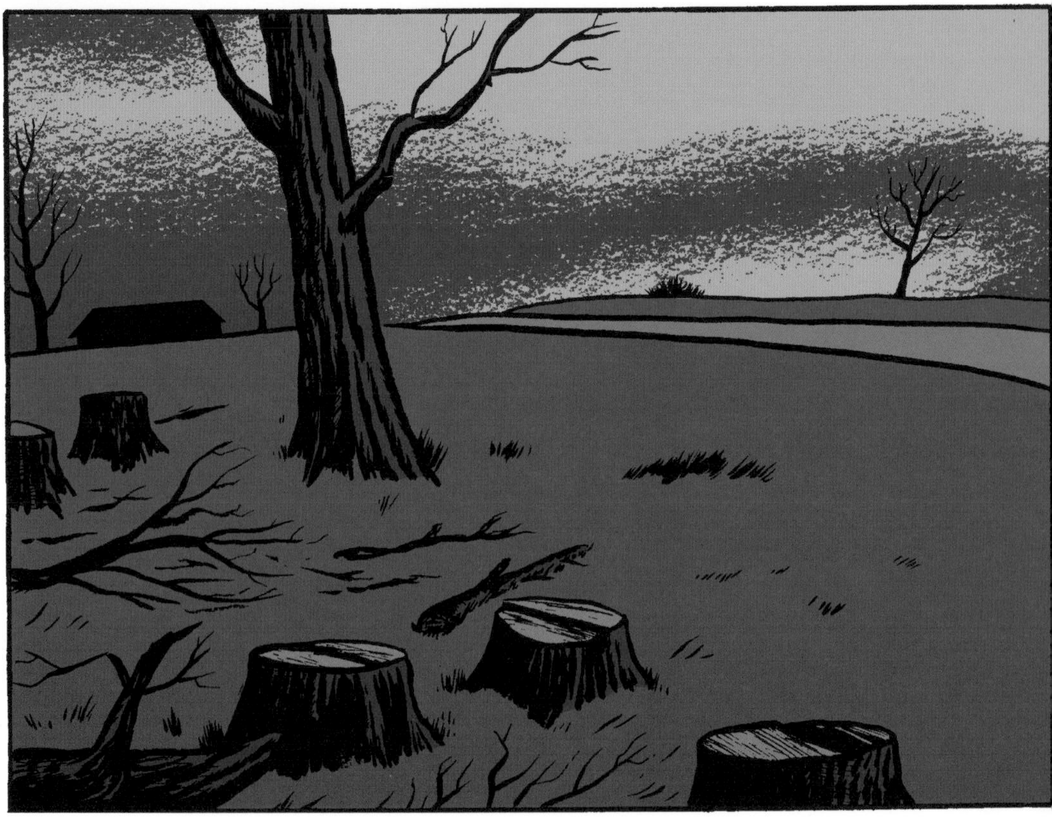

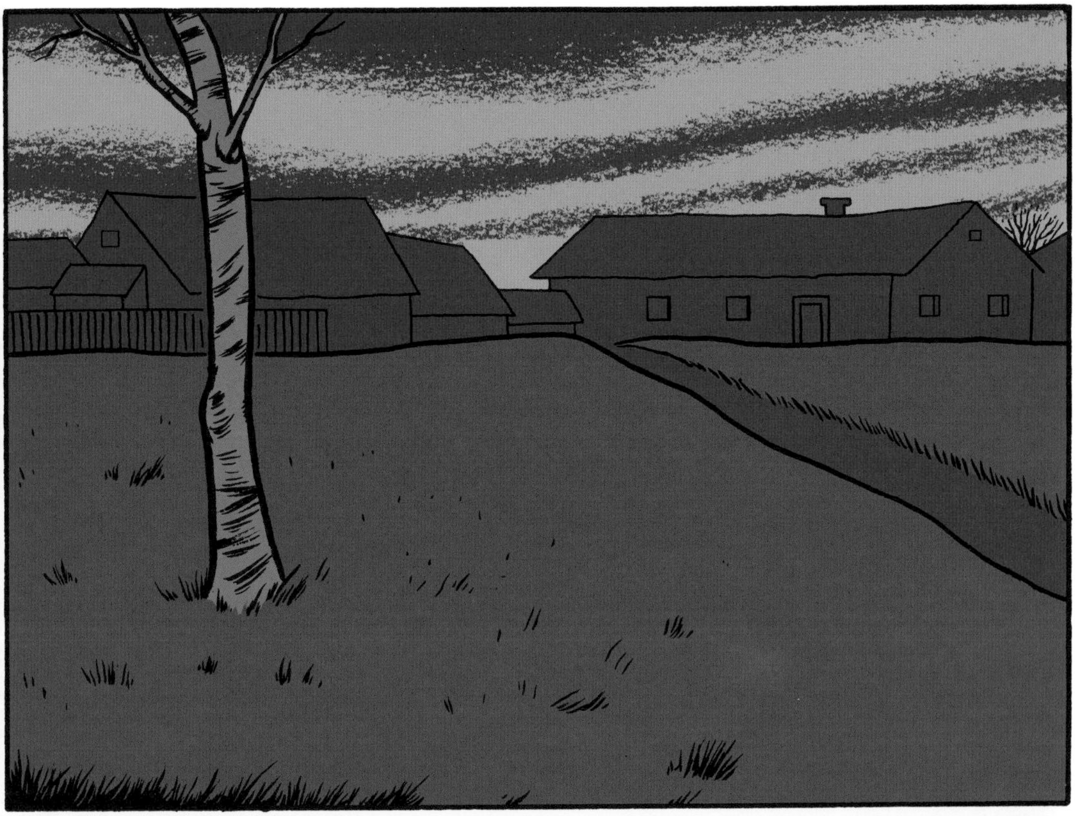

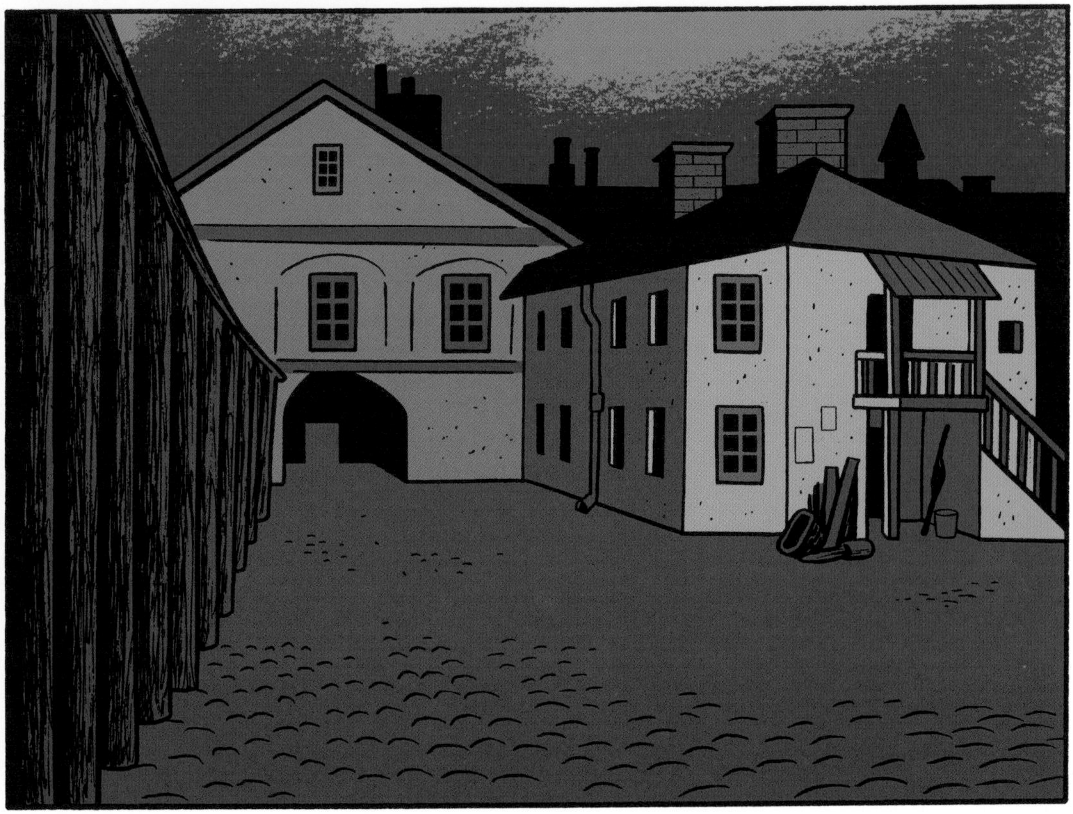

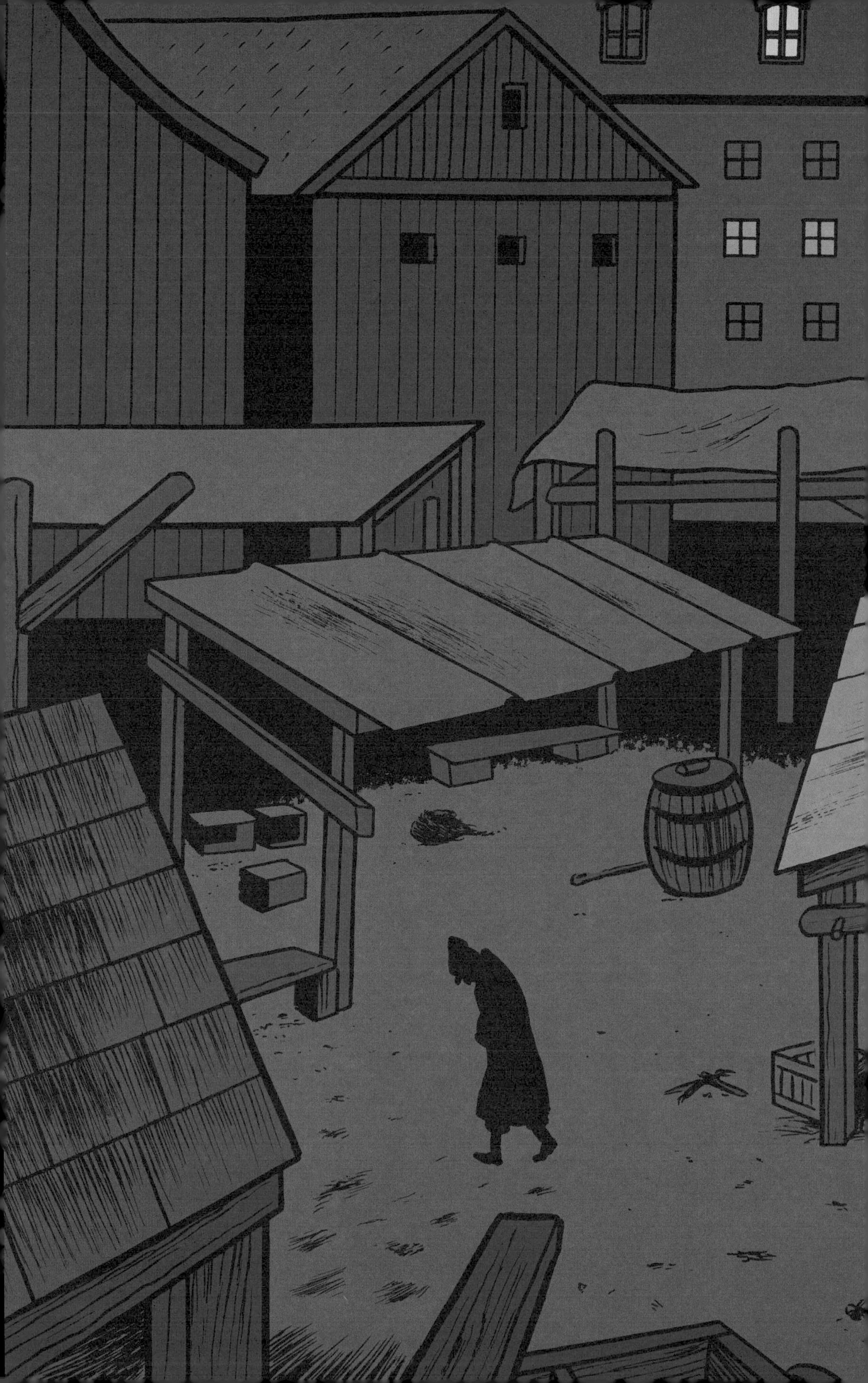

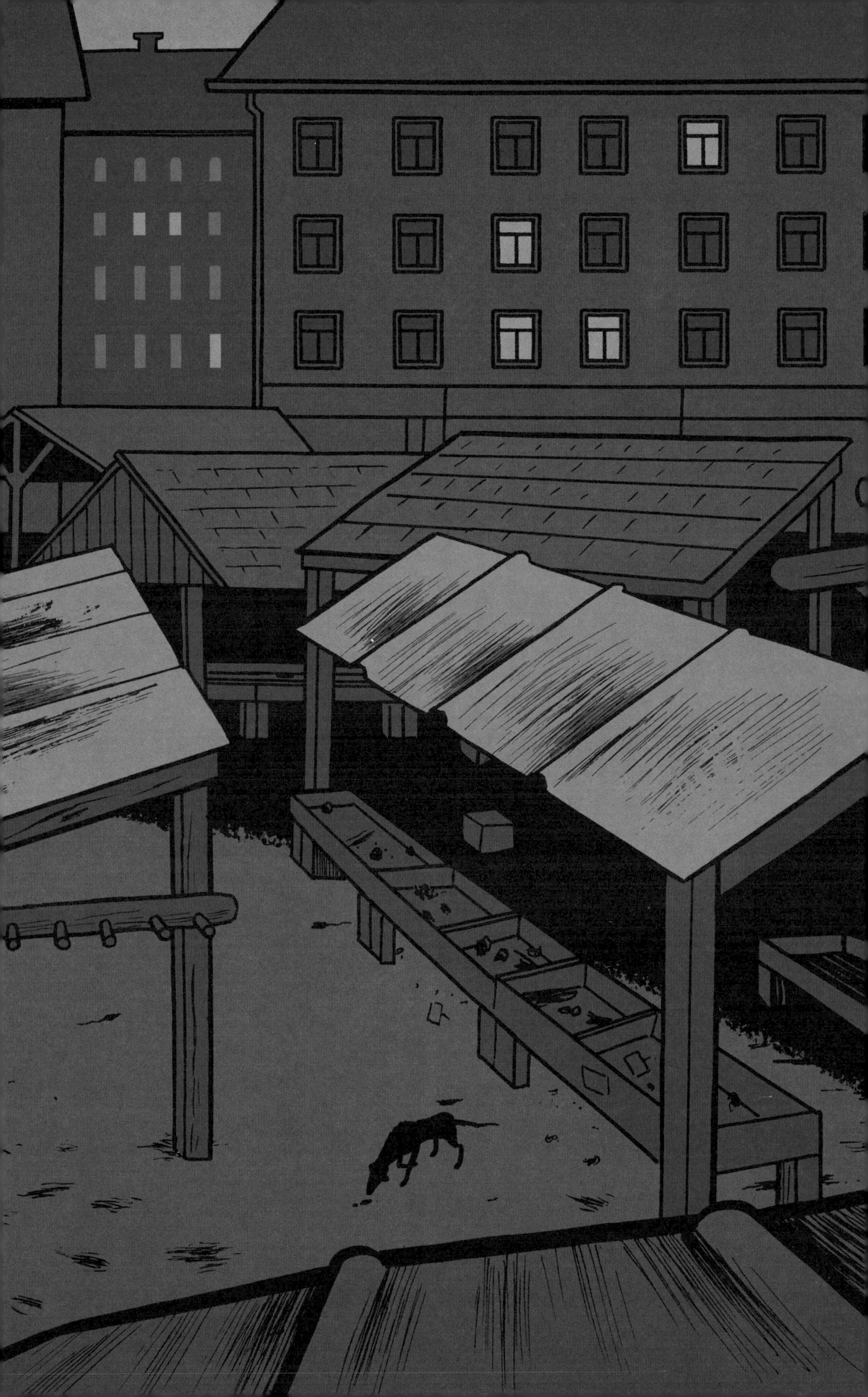

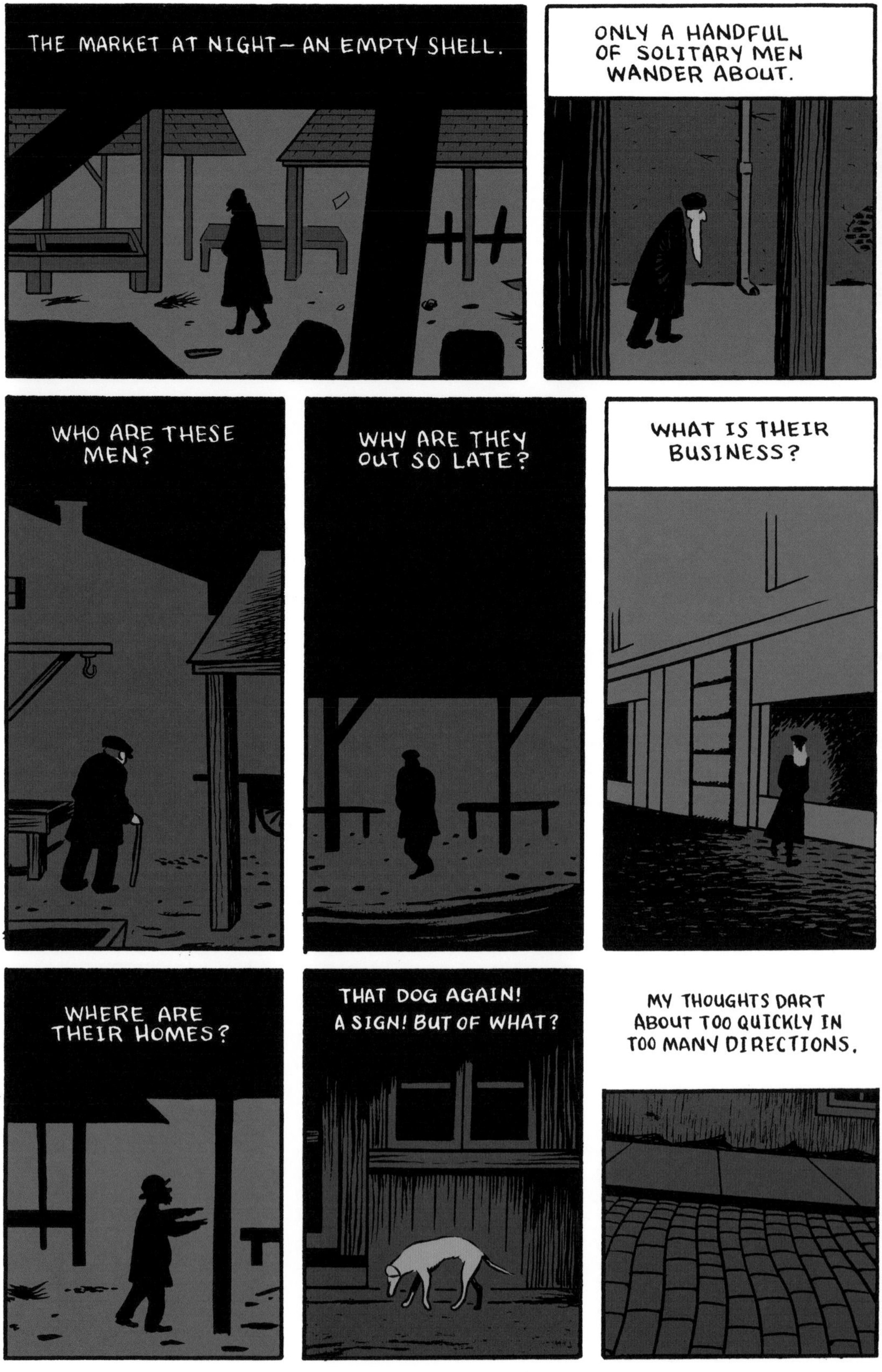
THE MARKET AT NIGHT— AN EMPTY SHELL.
ONLY A HANDFUL OF SOLITARY MEN WANDER ABOUT.
WHO ARE THESE MEN?
WHY ARE THEY OUT SO LATE?
WHAT IS THEIR BUSINESS?
WHERE ARE THEIR HOMES?
THAT DOG AGAIN!
A SIGN! BUT OF WHAT?
MY THOUGHTS DART ABOUT TOO QUICKLY IN TOO MANY DIRECTIONS.

I TRY COUNTING
FOOTSTEPS.

BUT THEY JUST LEAD ME TO AN ALLEY WHERE MENACING FORMS
EMERGE FROM STAINS AND SHADOWS.

HE UP
AND LEFT.

NO NOTICE,
NO WARNING.

A FINKLE

HOW NAIVE I AM!
FINKLER WASN'T FAMILY—
HE RAN A SHOP!

THE FORTUNE TELLER'S
WORDS NOW CONDEMN
ME TO EXILE.

GOD WILL REVEAL
HIMSELF THROUGH
YOUR WORK

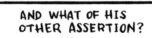

AND WHAT OF HIS
OTHER ASSERTION?

YOU ARE A
NEW FATHER

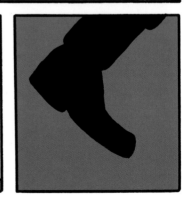

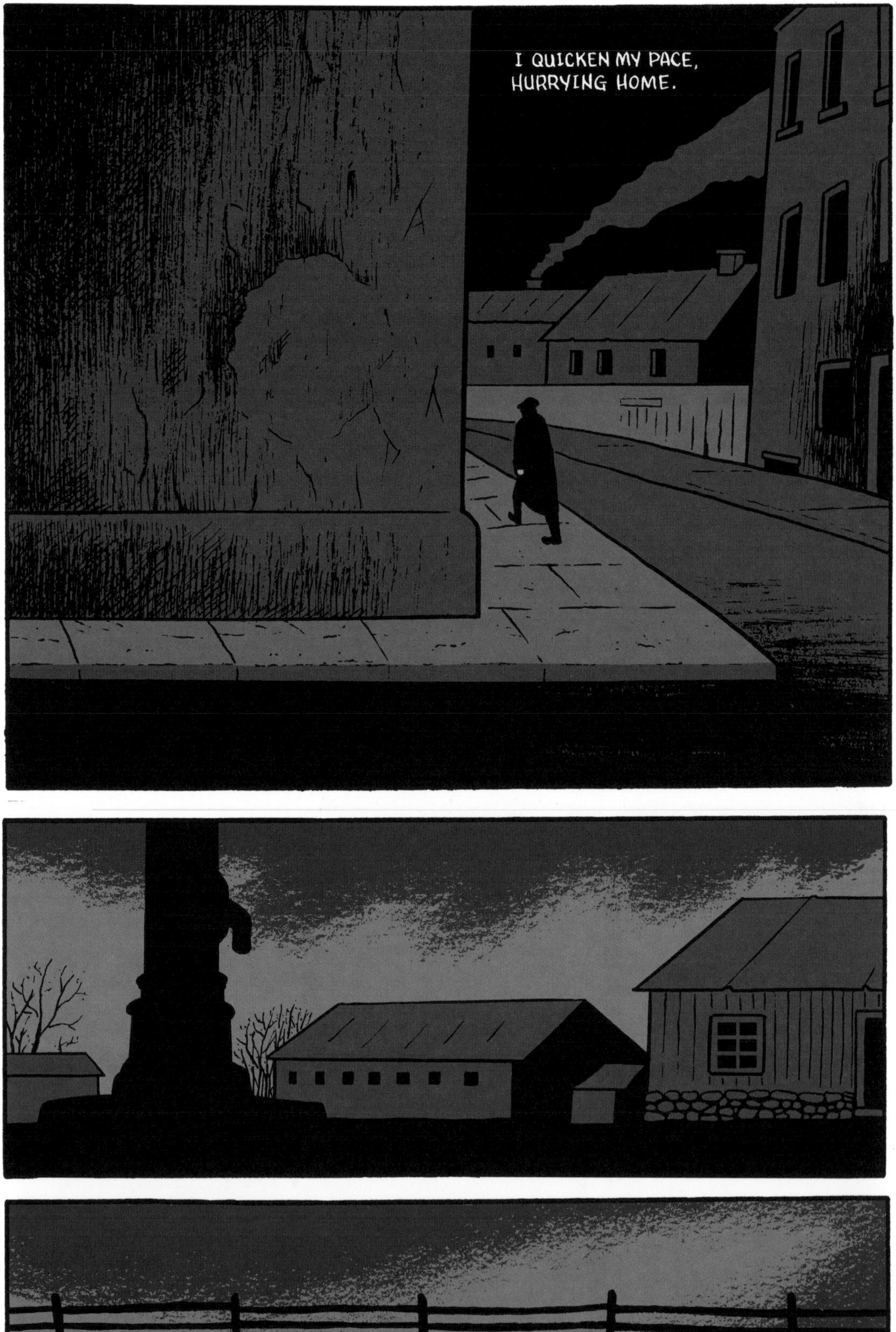
I QUICKEN MY PACE, HURRYING HOME.

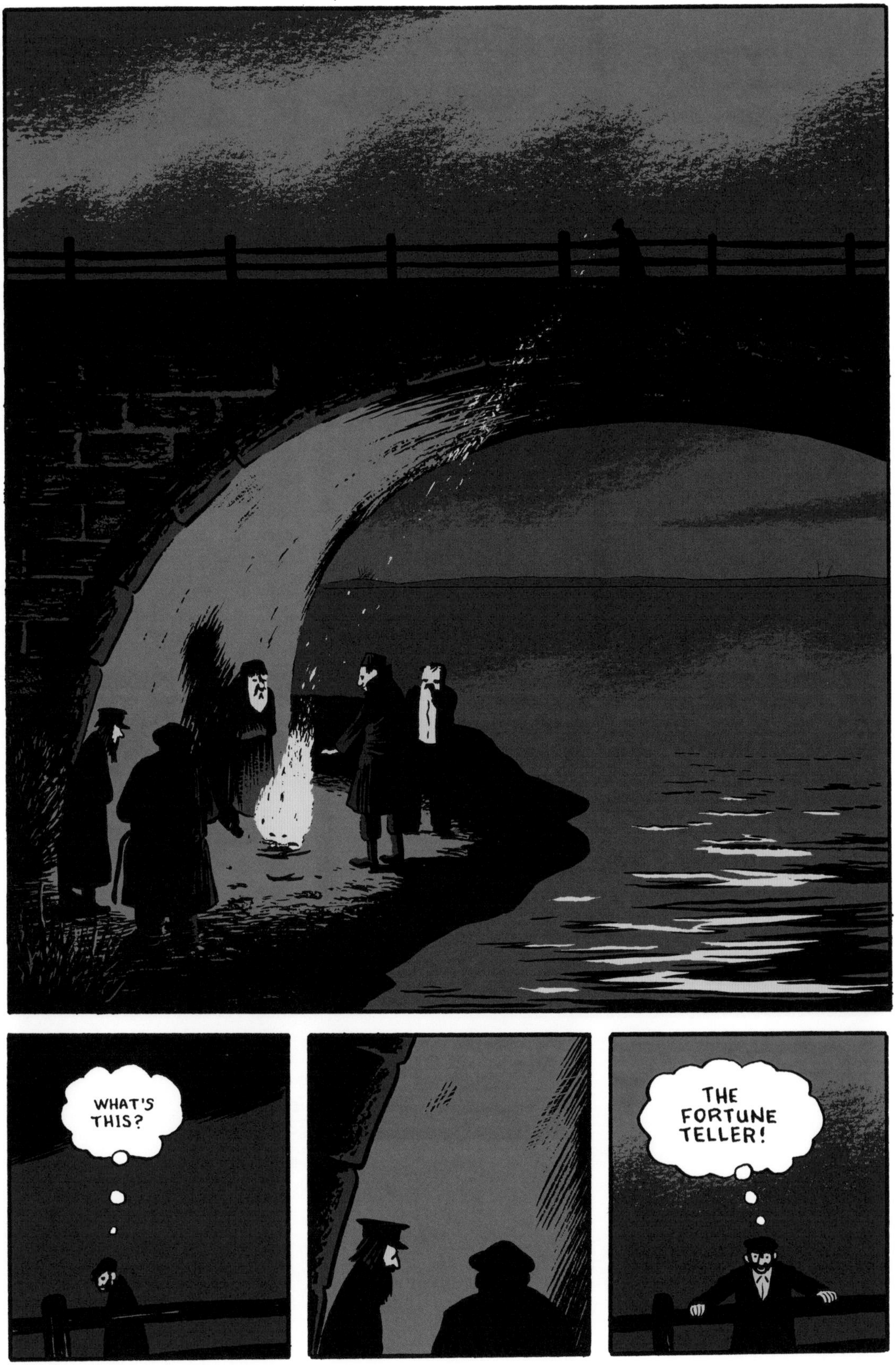
WHAT'S THIS?
THE FORTUNE TELLER!

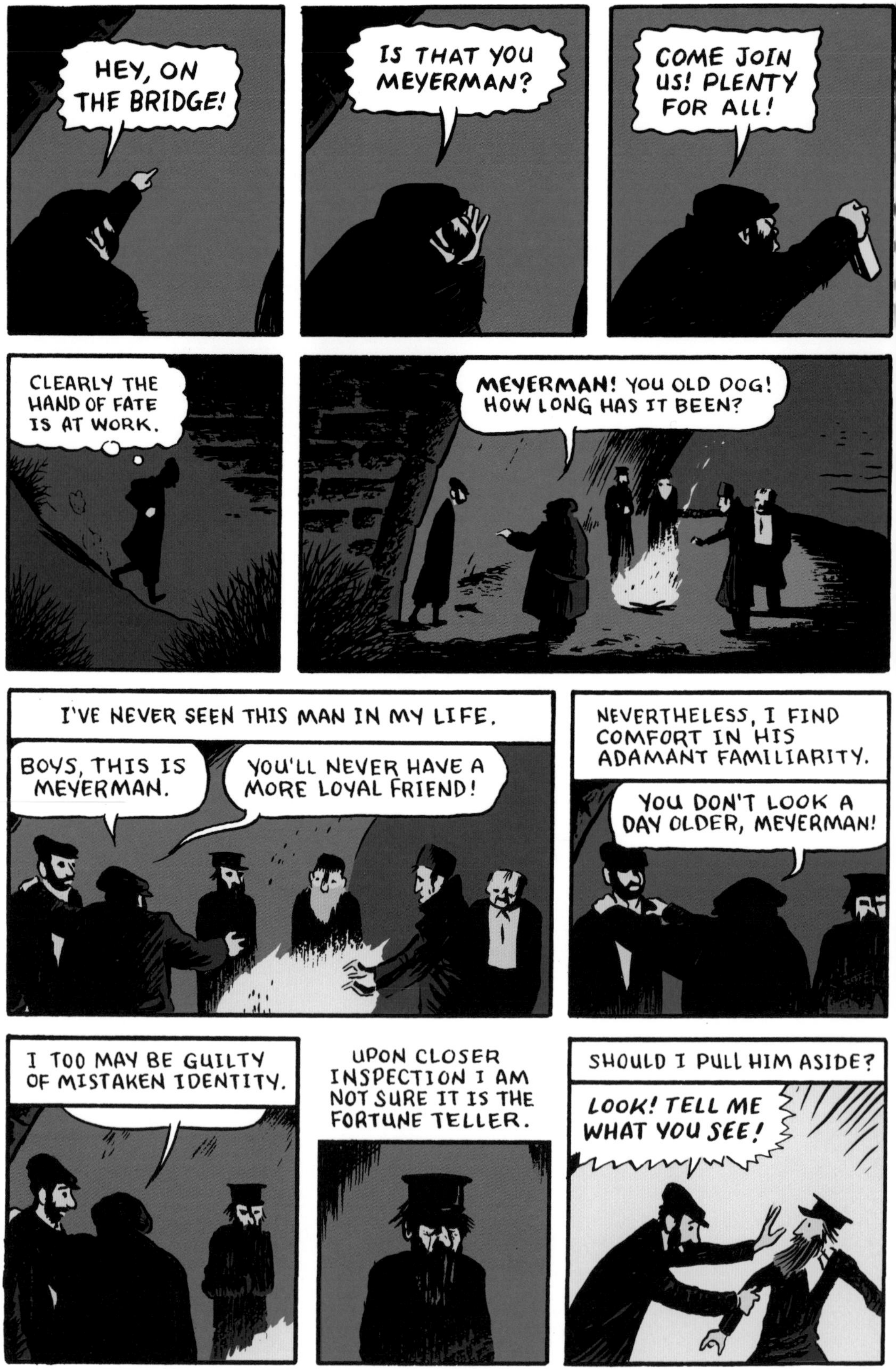
HEY, ON THE BRIDGE!
IS THAT YOU MEYERMAN?
COME JOIN US! PLENTY FOR ALL!
CLEARLY THE HAND OF FATE IS AT WORK.
MEYERMAN! YOU OLD DOG! HOW LONG HAS IT BEEN?
I'VE NEVER SEEN THIS MAN IN MY LIFE.
BOYS, THIS IS MEYERMAN.
YOU'LL NEVER HAVE A MORE LOYAL FRIEND!
NEVERTHELESS, I FIND COMFORT IN HIS ADAMANT FAMILIARITY.
YOU DON'T LOOK A DAY OLDER, MEYERMAN!
I TOO MAY BE GUILTY OF MISTAKEN IDENTITY.
UPON CLOSER INSPECTION I AM NOT SURE IT IS THE FORTUNE TELLER.
SHOULD I PULL HIM ASIDE?
LOOK! TELL ME WHAT YOU SEE!

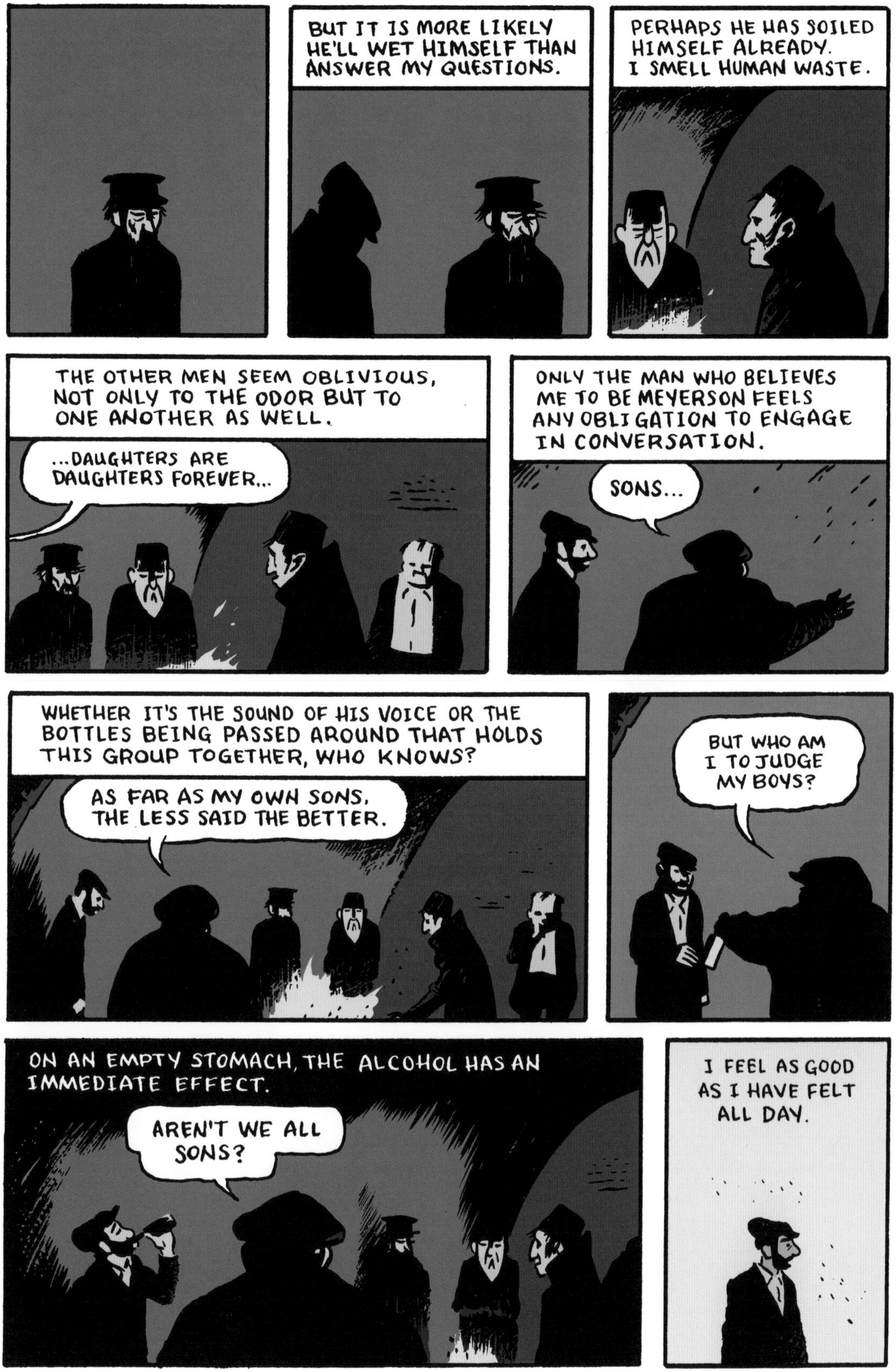
BUT IT IS MORE LIKELY HE'LL WET HIMSELF THAN ANSWER MY QUESTIONS.
PERHAPS HE HAS SOILED HIMSELF ALREADY. I SMELL HUMAN WASTE.
THE OTHER MEN SEEM OBLIVIOUS, NOT ONLY TO THE ODOR BUT TO ONE ANOTHER AS WELL.
...DAUGHTERS ARE DAUGHTERS FOREVER...
ONLY THE MAN WHO BELIEVES ME TO BE MEYERSON FEELS ANY OBLIGATION TO ENGAGE IN CONVERSATION.
SONS...
WHETHER IT'S THE SOUND OF HIS VOICE OR THE BOTTLES BEING PASSED AROUND THAT HOLDS THIS GROUP TOGETHER, WHO KNOWS?
AS FAR AS MY OWN SONS, THE LESS SAID THE BETTER.
BUT WHO AM I TO JUDGE MY BOYS?
ON AN EMPTY STOMACH, THE ALCOHOL HAS AN IMMEDIATE EFFECT.
AREN'T WE ALL SONS?
I FEEL AS GOOD AS I HAVE FELT ALL DAY.

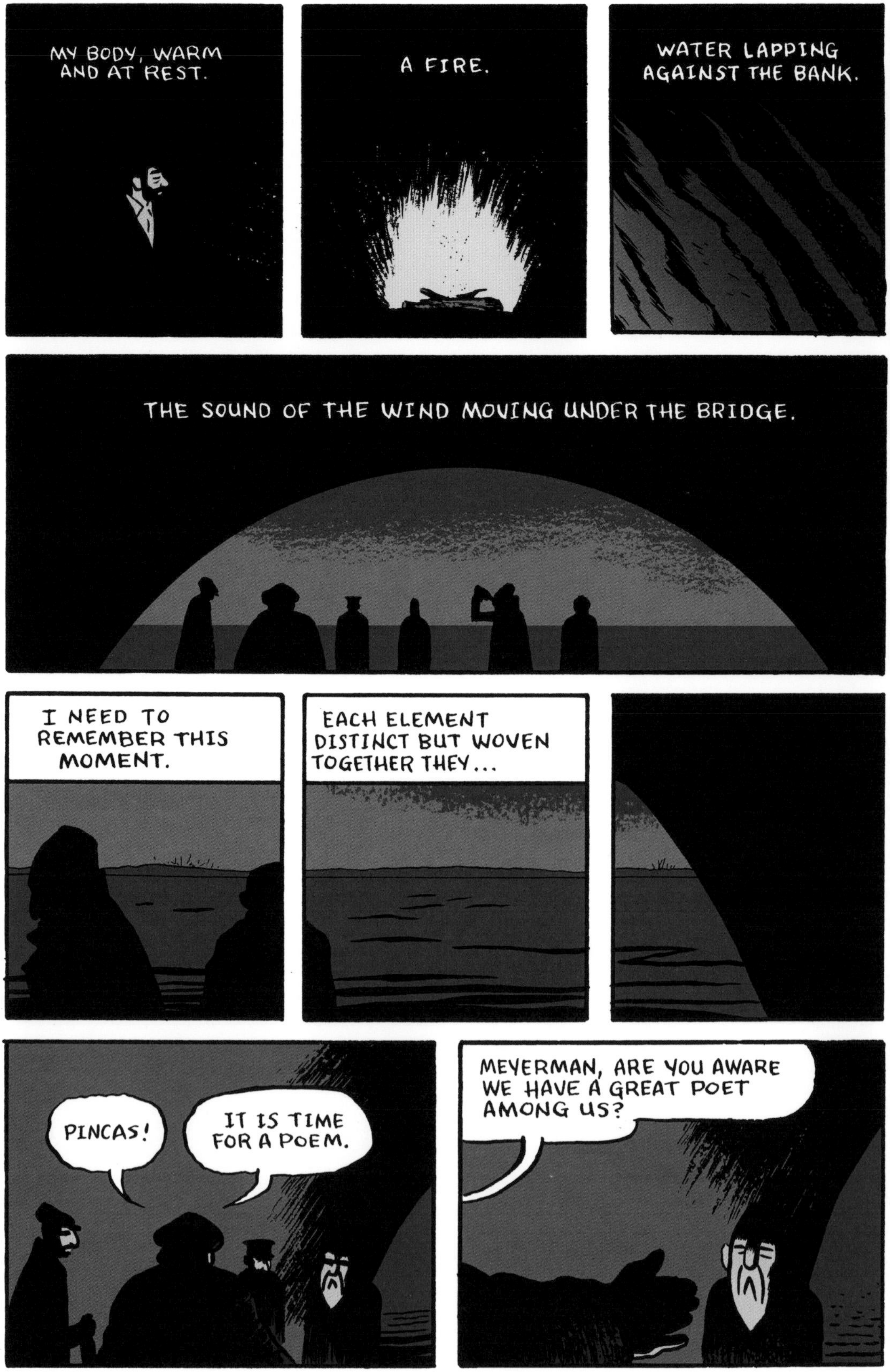
MY BODY, WARM AND AT REST.
A FIRE.
WATER LAPPING AGAINST THE BANK.
THE SOUND OF THE WIND MOVING UNDER THE BRIDGE.
I NEED TO REMEMBER THIS MOMENT.
EACH ELEMENT DISTINCT BUT WOVEN TOGETHER THEY...
PINCAS!
IT IS TIME FOR A POEM.
MEYERMAN, ARE YOU AWARE WE HAVE A GREAT POET AMONG US?

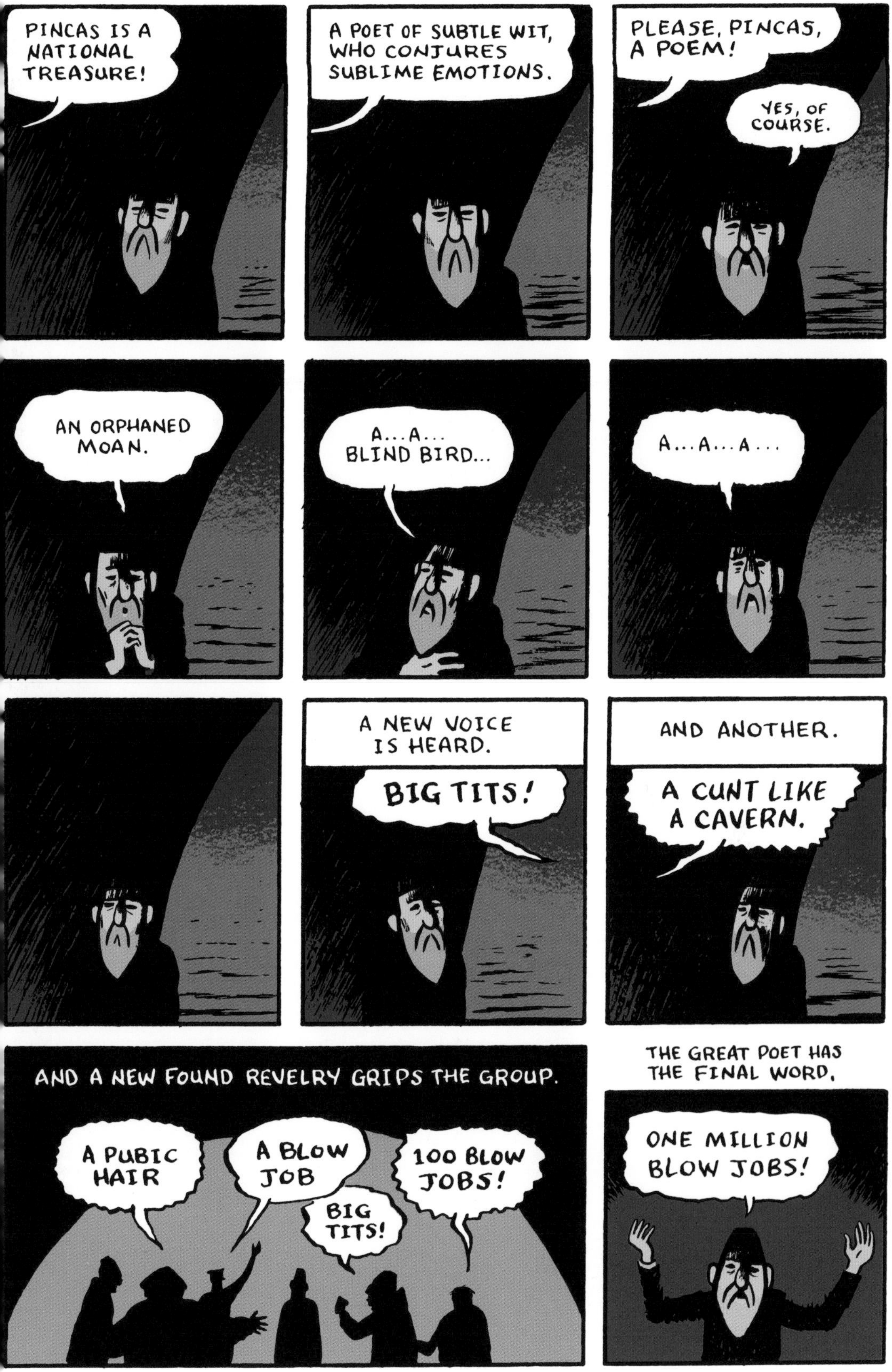
PINCAS IS A NATIONAL TREASURE!
A POET OF SUBTLE WIT, WHO CONJURES SUBLIME EMOTIONS.
PLEASE, PINCAS, A POEM!
YES, OF COURSE.
AN ORPHANED MOAN.
A... A... BLIND BIRD...
A... A... A...
A NEW VOICE IS HEARD.
BIG TITS!
AND ANOTHER.
A CUNT LIKE A CAVERN.
AND A NEW FOUND REVELRY GRIPS THE GROUP.
A PUBIC HAIR
A BLOW JOB
BIG TITS!
100 BLOW JOBS!
THE GREAT POET HAS THE FINAL WORD.
ONE MILLION BLOW JOBS!

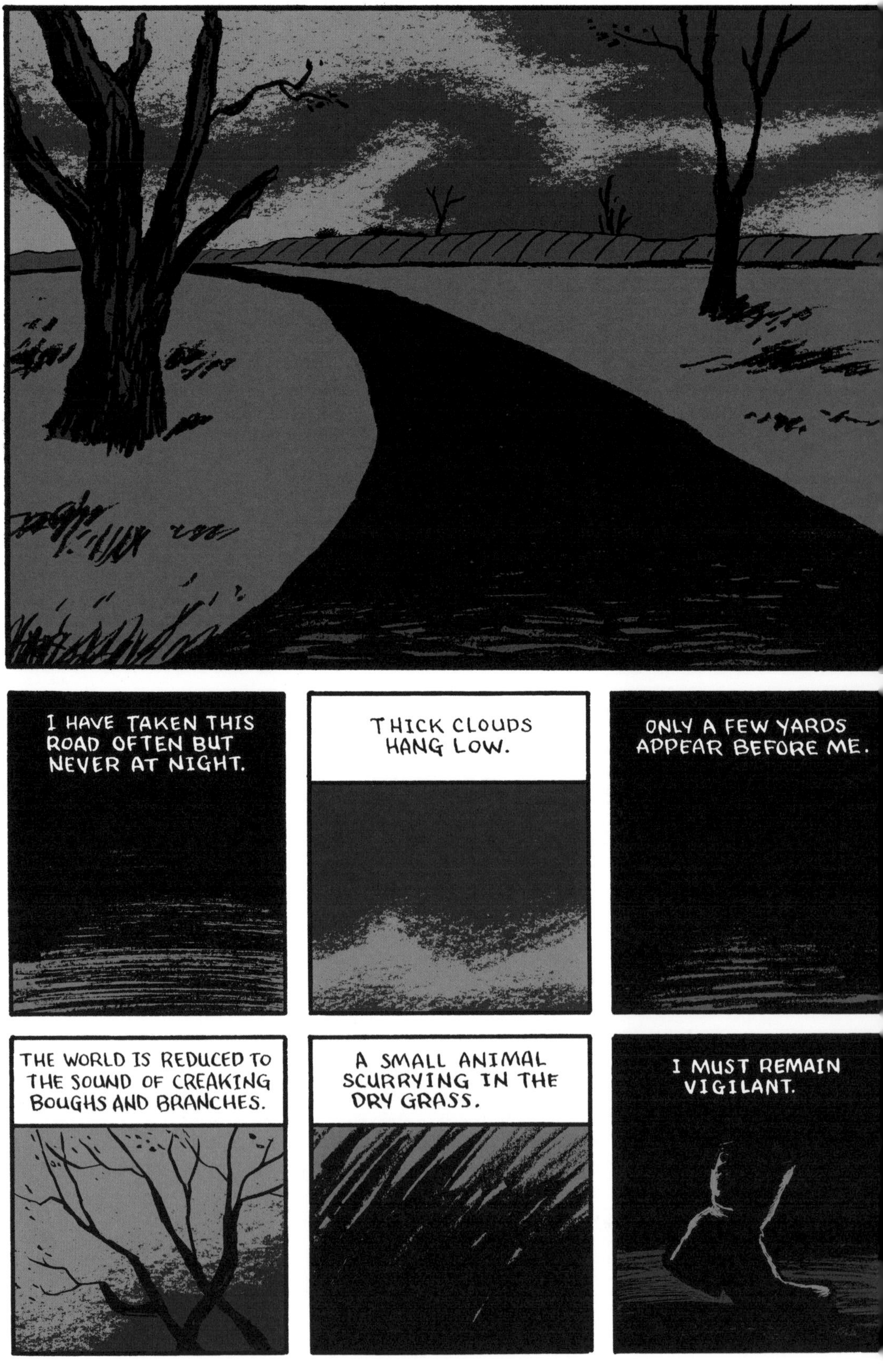
I HAVE TAKEN THIS ROAD OFTEN BUT NEVER AT NIGHT.
THICK CLOUDS HANG LOW.
ONLY A FEW YARDS APPEAR BEFORE ME.
THE WORLD IS REDUCED TO THE SOUND OF CREAKING BOUGHS AND BRANCHES.
A SMALL ANIMAL SCURRYING IN THE DRY GRASS.
I MUST REMAIN VIGILANT.

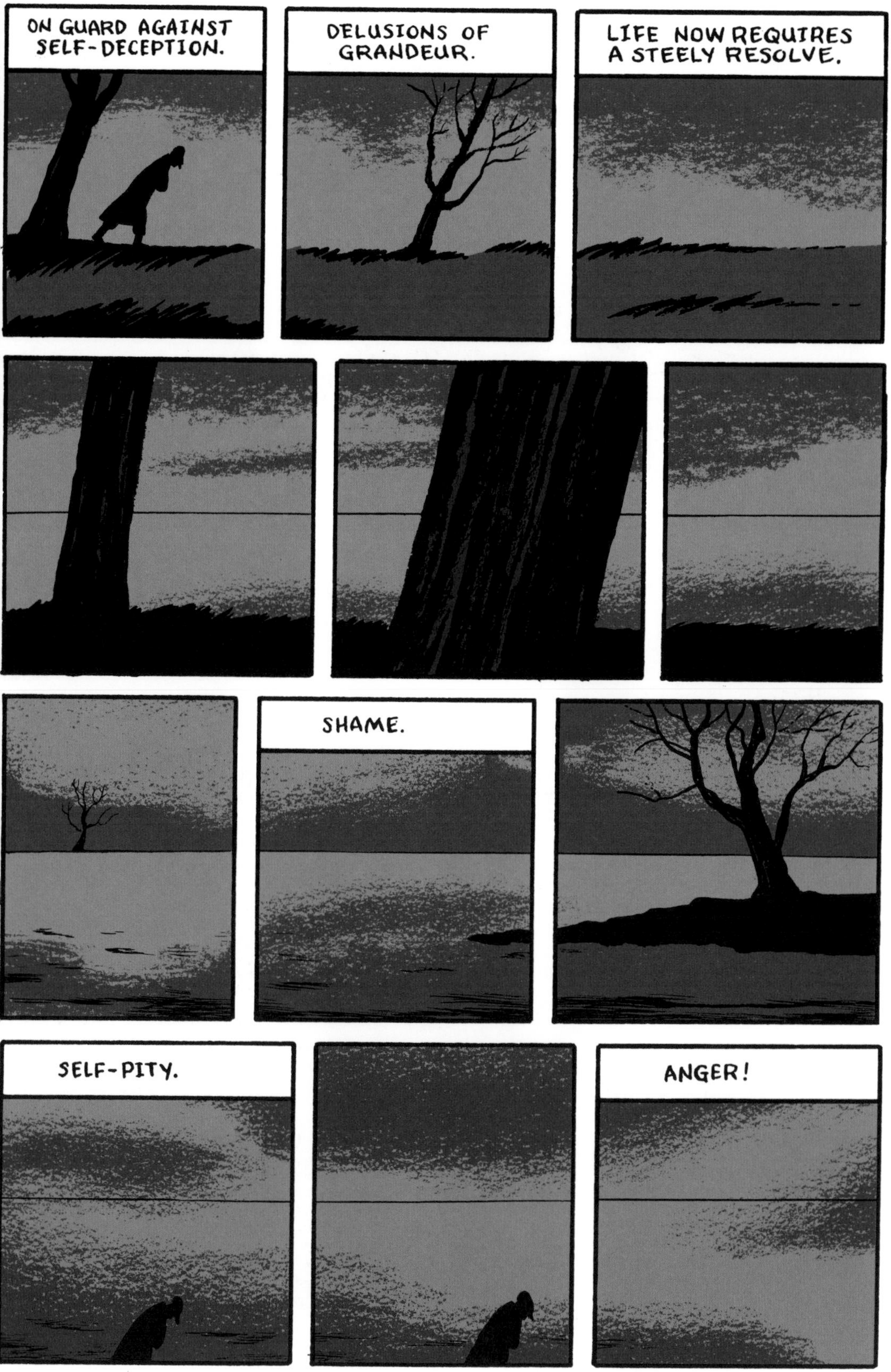
ON GUARD AGAINST SELF-DECEPTION.
DELUSIONS OF GRANDEUR.
LIFE NOW REQUIRES A STEELY RESOLVE.
SHAME.
SELF-PITY.
ANGER!

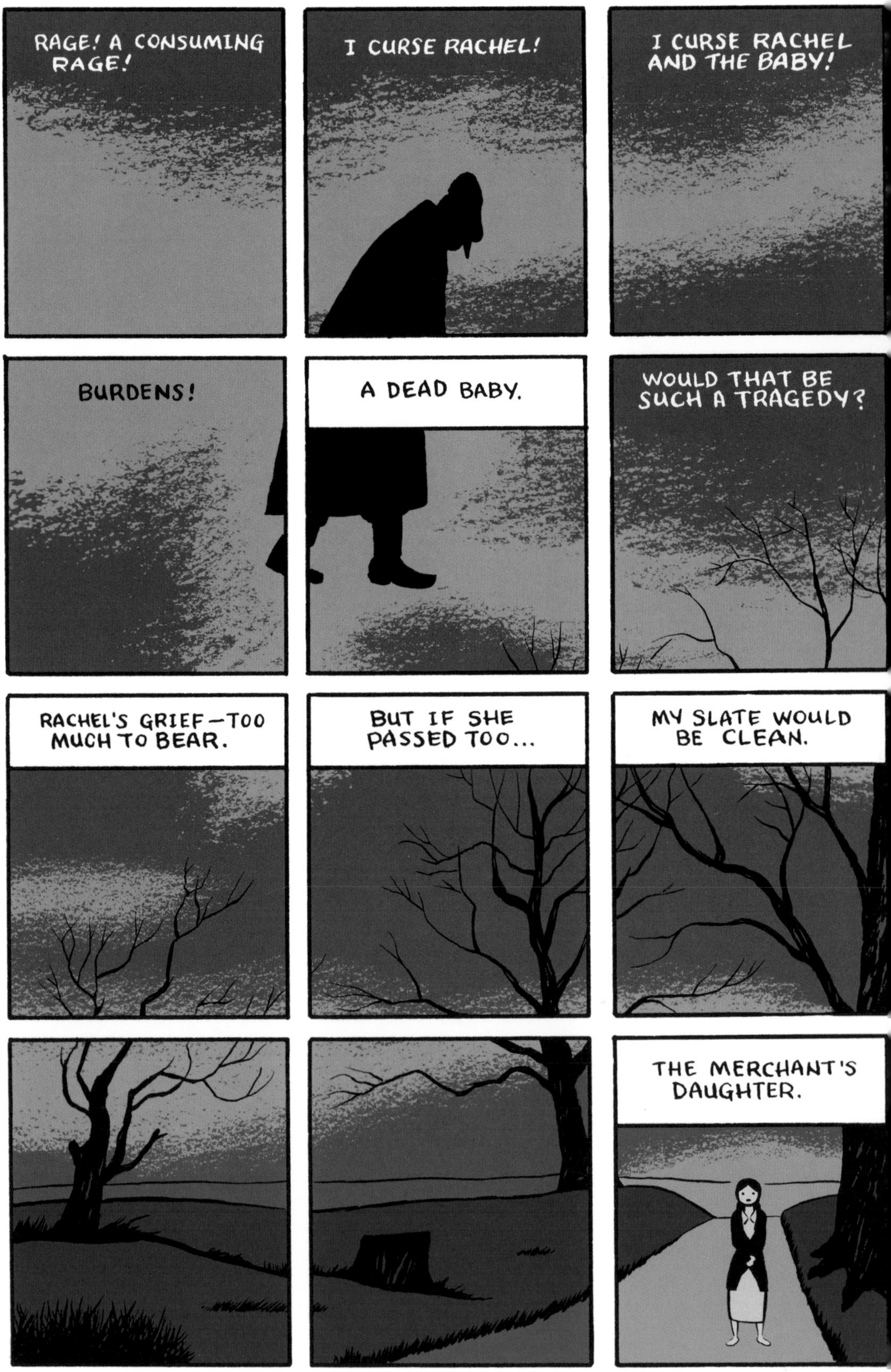
RAGE! A CONSUMING RAGE!
I CURSE RACHEL!
I CURSE RACHEL AND THE BABY!
BURDENS!
A DEAD BABY.
WOULD THAT BE SUCH A TRAGEDY?
RACHEL'S GRIEF—TOO MUCH TO BEAR.
BUT IF SHE PASSED TOO...
MY SLATE WOULD BE CLEAN.
THE MERCHANT'S DAUGHTER.

EVEN AS HER FATHER REJECTED ME, HER BEAUTY CAUGHT MY EYE.

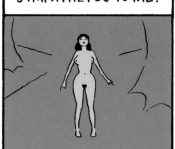
I COULD TELL BY HER LOOK, SHE WOULD BE SYMPATHETIC TO ME.

PERHAPS WE WOULD START A NEW LIFE TOGETHER...

SUCH THOUGHTS! SUCH MONSTROUS DEPRAVED THOUGHTS!

HOW MUCH FURTHER?

SO TIRED.

JUST FOR A MOMENT...

A SHORT REST.

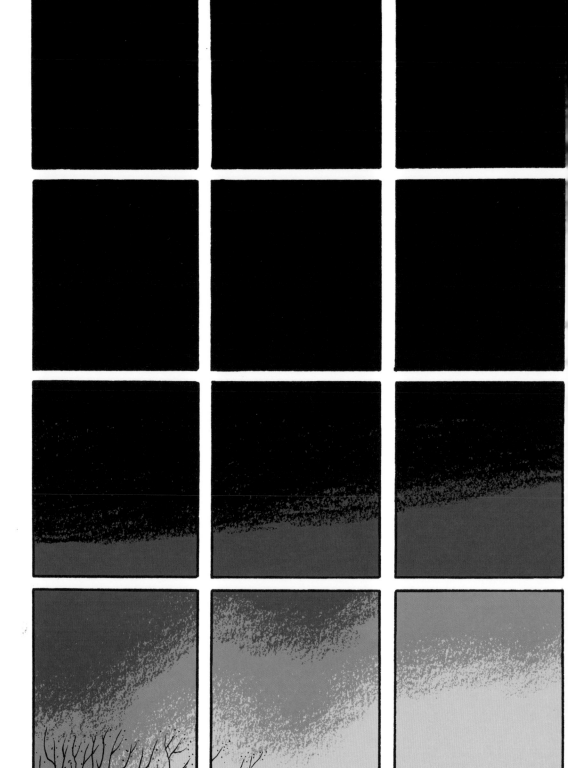

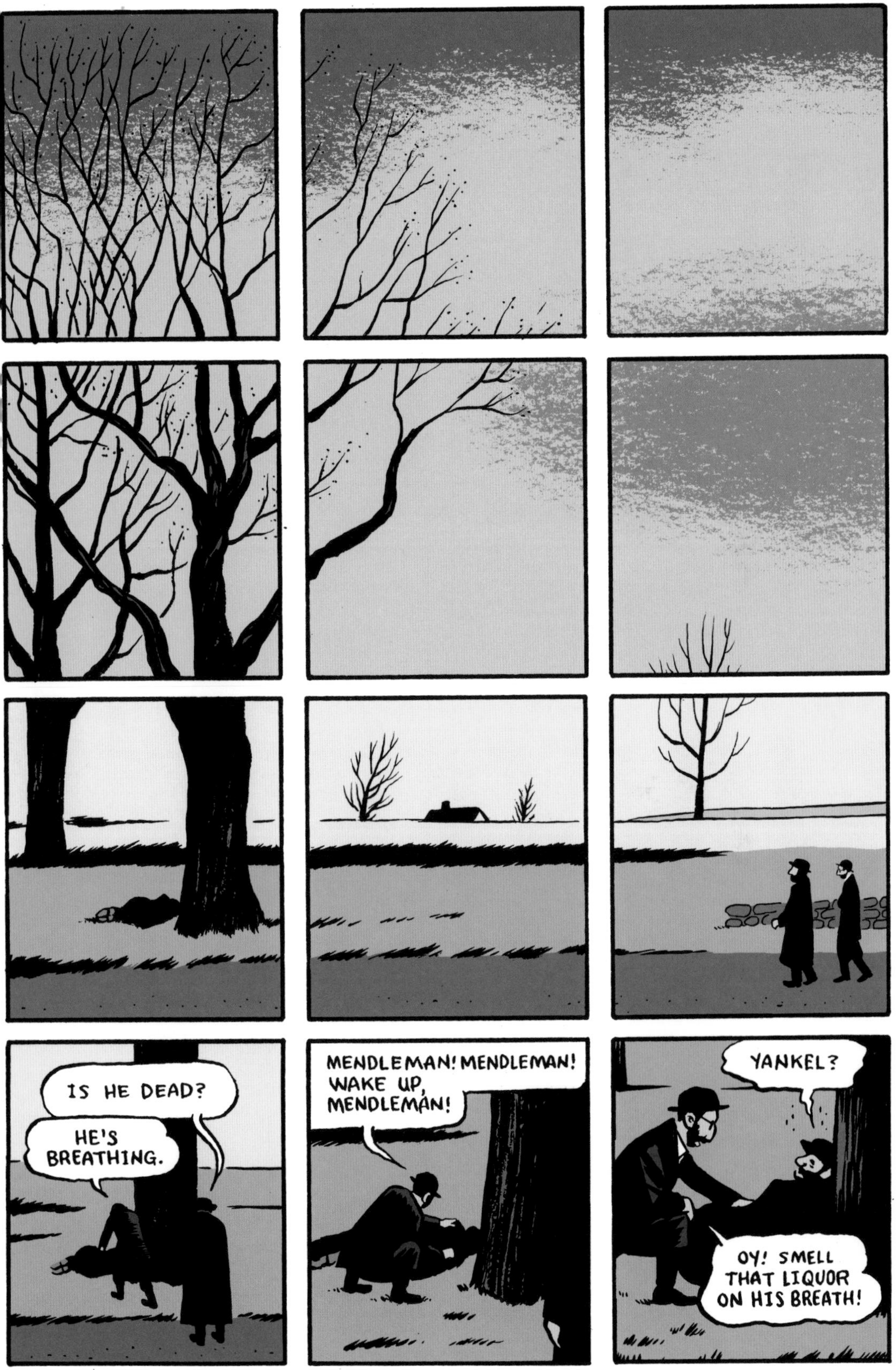
IS HE DEAD?
HE'S BREATHING.
MENDLEMAN! MENDLEMAN! WAKE UP, MENDLEMAN!
YANKEL?
OY! SMELL THAT LIQUOR ON HIS BREATH!

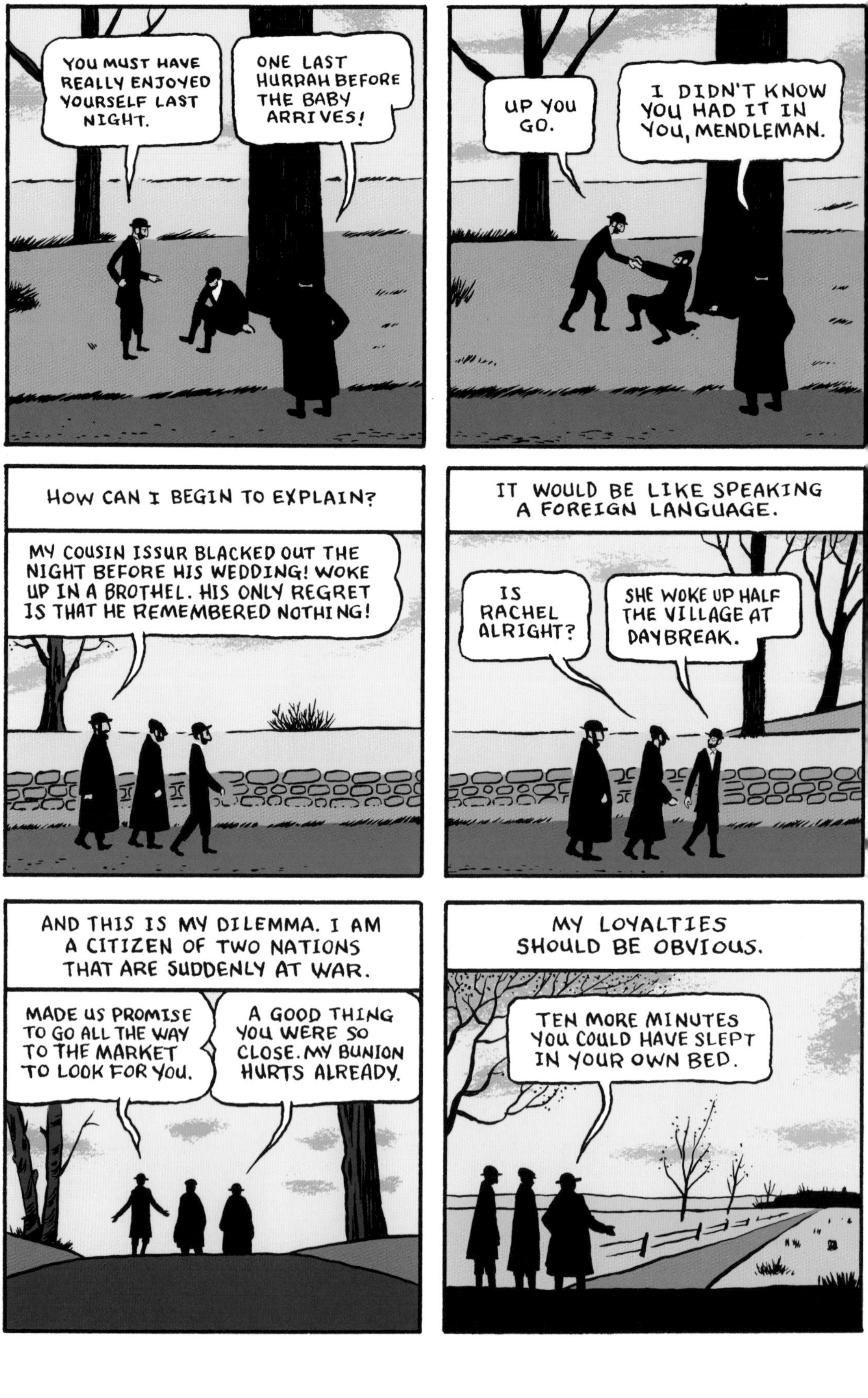
YOU MUST HAVE REALLY ENJOYED YOURSELF LAST NIGHT.
ONE LAST HURRAH BEFORE THE BABY ARRIVES!
UP YOU GO.
I DIDN'T KNOW YOU HAD IT IN YOU, MENDLEMAN.
HOW CAN I BEGIN TO EXPLAIN?
MY COUSIN ISSUR BLACKED OUT THE NIGHT BEFORE HIS WEDDING! WOKE UP IN A BROTHEL. HIS ONLY REGRET IS THAT HE REMEMBERED NOTHING!
IT WOULD BE LIKE SPEAKING A FOREIGN LANGUAGE.
IS RACHEL ALRIGHT?
SHE WOKE UP HALF THE VILLAGE AT DAYBREAK.
AND THIS IS MY DILEMMA. I AM A CITIZEN OF TWO NATIONS THAT ARE SUDDENLY AT WAR.
MADE US PROMISE TO GO ALL THE WAY TO THE MARKET TO LOOK FOR YOU.
A GOOD THING YOU WERE SO CLOSE. MY BUNION HURTS ALREADY.
MY LOYALTIES SHOULD BE OBVIOUS.
TEN MORE MINUTES YOU COULD HAVE SLEPT IN YOUR OWN BED.

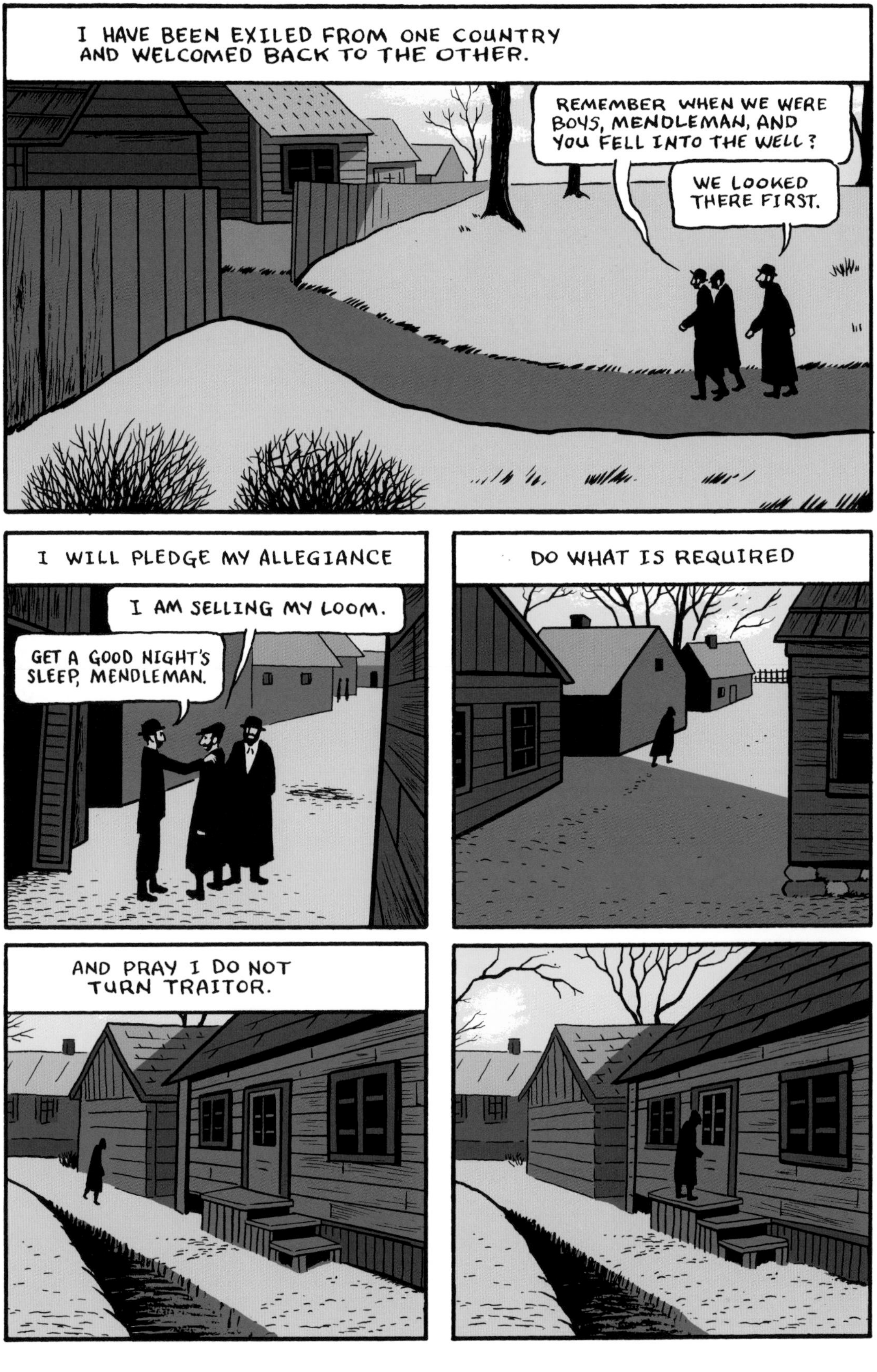
I HAVE BEEN EXILED FROM ONE COUNTRY AND WELCOMED BACK TO THE OTHER.
REMEMBER WHEN WE WERE BOYS, MENDLEMAN, AND YOU FELL INTO THE WELL?
WE LOOKED THERE FIRST.
I WILL PLEDGE MY ALLEGIANCE
I AM SELLING MY LOOM.
GET A GOOD NIGHT'S SLEEP, MENDLEMAN.
DO WHAT IS REQUIRED
AND PRAY I DO NOT TURN TRAITOR.

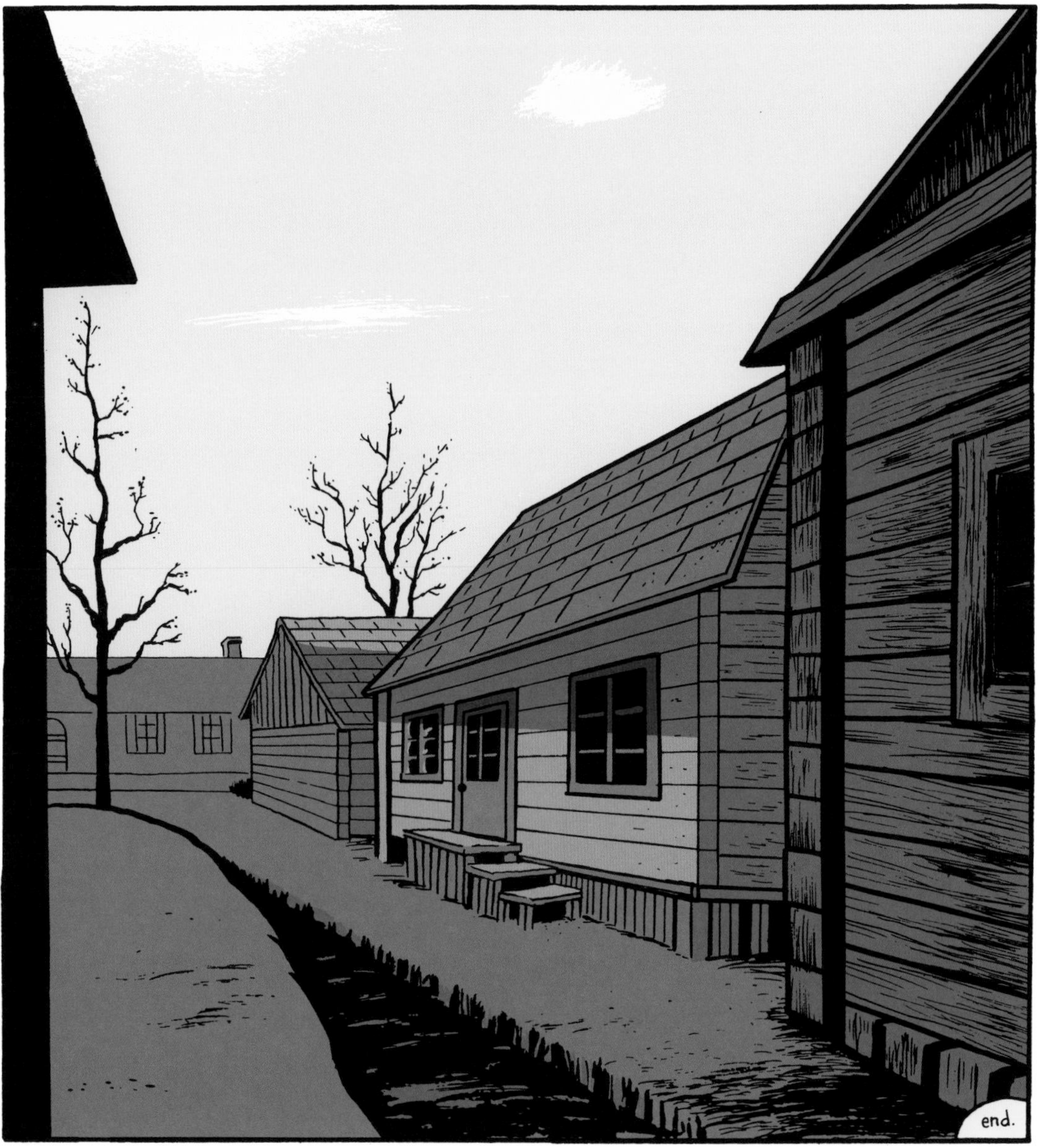
end.

ACKNOWLEDGEMENTS

The photographs of Roman Vishniac and Alter Kacyzne,
the postcard collection of Gerard Silvain (featured in the book YIDDISHLAND),
and the drawings of Lionel S. Reiss and Denys Wortman provided invaluable reference and inspiration.

Thanks to the MacDowell Colony for recharging my creative battery.
It was the ideal setting to work on MARKET DAY.

This book is dedicated to my fellow cartoonists and Michelle Ollie.